SURVIVOR

THE UNOFFICIAL BIBLE OF THE

GREATEST REALITY SHOW EVER MADE

To My Beautiful Wife Allison and My Wonderful Son Ryan. Life Is So Much Better With You Two By My Side.

INTRODUCTION

"The tribe has spoken." Those four simple words have become a well-embedded phrase in the pop culture world and they were first uttered by a young, unknown television reality show host by the name of Jeff Probst. The show was called Survivor and it first appeared during the summer of 2000 in order to fill some vacant prime time television slots for CBS since their anchor programs were on summer hiatus. Part social experiment, part call to the wild, part morbid curiosity, the inaugural Survivor Borneo series became an overnight sensation that has now spanned 23 seasons and over 400 players from all walks of life. Husbands, wives, mothers, fathers, college students, senior citizens, amputees, hearing impaired, famous sports celebrities, and much more have populated the various tribes over the decade-plus Survivor has resided in the television landscape with seemingly no end in sight from all of the fun. No doubt even producer Mark Burnett couldn't have envisioned how much of a hit he had on his hands when the original Pagong and Tagi tribes hit the beach and an arrogant Richard Hatch, who of course would go on to be the very first Survivor million dollar winner, arrogantly (and correctly it turned out) proclaimed that he was already the winner before the game even got started. In the end 51.7 million smitten fans tuned in to the

Borneo finale and CBS honchos tripped all over themselves in ordering more seasons from Burnett. Just to cement how Survivor had officially reached the big time almost overnight, the following installment, Survivor the Australian Outback, debuted right after none other than the biggest sporting even in the nation, the Super Bowl. Survivor was here to stay and has become a cultural and television phenomenon that continues to endure and outlive even the most optimistic boosters.

As one of those fans who was bitten by the Survivor bug way back in that summer of 2000, I have been along for the ride every single step of the way. I have watched every second of every single season and thus the birth of "Survivor: The Unofficial Bible To The Greatest Reality Show Ever" was born. Allow me to take you all down memory lane as I revisit some of the very best and most controversial players who ever stepped foot into the Survivor world. Who truly was the best Survivor player ever? Who was overrated? Who should have or should not have won their season? In addition, I will look back at some of the biggest and boldest Survivor gimmicks throughout the years and dissect which ones were keepers and which ones fell flat on their face, along with noteworthy injuries, romances, and celebrity participants.

Finally, I will delve into the game itself from a so-called expert's perspective (that expert being me) and share with you what I think is the

optimum strategy needed to collect the million dollars, along with the biggest

mistakes that players in the past have made to augment their ouster from the

tribe. Consider this book part armchair quarterback, part television critic, and

part Survivor historical reference. It will be a fun ride I promise you.

CHAPTER 1: THE BEST OF THE BEST

ROB MARIANO

Survivor Seasons (4): Marquesas, All Stars, Heroes VS. Villains,

Redemption Island

Titles: Redemption Island

Biggest Rival: Russell Hantz

Claim To Fame Besides Winning: Marrying All Stars Winner Amber

Brkitch

Rob "Boston Rob" Mariano was destined to be on Survivor. The

tough guy Italian with the heavy 'Bawston' accent had a self-confidence and

odd sense of humor that made him an instant hit when he debuted on season 4

in Marquesas. Playing his initial Survivor game with a great deal of outward

bravado and gusto, Rob immediately went to work in forming an alliance in

his Maraamu tribe as he seemed to be putting himself into a big time power

position. However a tribal switch threw a huge monkey wrench into his plans

as he was sent to the opposing Rotu tribe where he ended up on the wrong

side of the numbers. Thus when the merge arrived, Rob was sent home first out of the final ten as his original Maraamu tribe was down 7 members to 3 against the Rotu. Despite the earlier than expected ouster, Rob was arguably the star of the season as he stole almost all of the scenes he was in with his outspoken nature. He also made a friendship with Kathy Vavrick-O'Brien who he would play the game with later on during All Stars.

Rob was recast for that All Star season which was the tenth installment of Survivor which, like in Australia, would debut with much hype after the Super Bowl. 18 former players were back in action and this time around the tribes were split into three groups of six. Rob's Chapera tribe was made up of Sue Hawk (Borneo), Tom "Big Tom" Buchannan (Africa), Rob Cesternino (Amazon), Alicia Callaway (Australia), and a young female by the name of Amber Brkitch (Australia). Right off the bat he made a quick pact with Amber, with her beauty being the first reason Rob mentioned for why he picked her. Rob immediately surmised that Rob C. was the biggest threat in his tribe due to his past as a devious schemer during his Amazon season and thus he engineered the first blindside of the game when he quickly stabbed him in he back after shaking hands on an alliance the day before.

Rob was just getting started at that point however as he quickly brought in two more alliance members in the form of Rupert Boneham and Jenna Lewis who came over after their tribe was dissolved in the first big twist of the game. At the same time, Rob and Amber were making headway on their blossoming romance as they shared an embrace which further solidified their alliance.

Meanwhile Rob was constantly strategizing and leading the way in challenges, with a body slam of Colby Donaldson into the water during an early immunity challenge being a clear highlight. However his game was threatened for the first time when for the second occasion in two seasons, a tribal switch sent him to the opposing team. Joining Rob was the rest of the Chapera tribe. All but Amber that is. Knowing that his game was not seriously in trouble, Rob proceeded to pitch a deal with Lex Van Den Burg (Africa), claiming that he would look out for him if he protected Amber from that night's tribal council. With O'Brien also on the new Chapera tribe with Lex and Amber, Rob was able to successfully hoodwink them both into following along with his plan which of course had a very ugly ending. Ultimately Lex came through for Rob and protected Amber from elimination in that subsequent tribal council (sending Jerry Manthey home instead) and afterwards the tribes merged. Right away Lex went to Rob to discuss the deal as another tribal council beckoned. Completely going back on his word for all to see, Rob told Lex he couldn't help him which infuriated the tattooed rocker. Meanwhile Kathy sat there the whole time crying over how she felt extremely betrayed by Rob after seemingly forming a bond with him while in Marquesas. Rob however was going full bore for the million dollars and there were no friends in his game. Well except for Amber that is who was quickly becoming more than a friend.

Once Lex and Kathy were out of the way, Rob was now in total control and he wasn't about to let anyone move in on his power. He covered his bases anyway by making a side deal with Callaway and than quickly stabbed her in the back as well in favor of staying the course with Amber, Rupert, and Jenna. When it got down to the final five, Rob pulled off one more bit of deception when he started a fight between Tom and Rupert in order to create the divide that would take attention away from himself and Amber. Add to that his successful convincing of Jenna to turn her back on Rupert at the final four so as not to have to deal with a 2-2 tie at the second to last TC, and Rob no doubt clinched the title of best game player by far in All Stars.

The next day, Jenna bit the dust in the last All Star challenge and Rob and Amber were in the finals. The final TC beckoned and no doubt sparks were going to fly due to all of the bodies Rob laid on the road on his way to the finals. Even Rob couldn't have predicted how nasty things would get in front of the jury however as one of the most ruthless final TC's ever was centered mostly on the jury absolutely destroying Rob with some very rough commentary. The highlight was Big Tom seemingly looking to bury the hatchet with Rob by approaching to shake hands in a let bygones be bygones gesture, At the last second however, Tom swipes his hand away and utters his infamous "Don't be stupid, stupid" comment which completely caught Rob and Amber off guard. After having Kathy cry in front of him as she delved into how hurt she was that Rob betrayed her the way he did and than have Lex absolutely destroy him as well, the look of shock and embarrassment on he and Amber's face was impossible to hide. By the end of the jury segment, Rob was visibly distressed and for the first time almost at a loss for words. The fact of the matter however was that the show had to go on and either he or Amber was going to be a millionaire and be given the title as the winner of Survivor All Stars.

A few months later when the results were to be read live, Rob made it a point to get some business out of the way before the votes were revealed. In order to eliminate the scenario of critics saying he only did it to ensure he was a millionaire if he lost the final vote tally, Rob got on one knee in front of the nation and proposed marriage to Amber who quickly accepted. With the proposal still hanging in the air, the reading of the votes was almost anti-climactic which revealed Amber to be the winner by a 4-3 tally. Still Rob made out all right by getting the girl and eventually sharing in that million dollars once they officially tied the knot a year later.

Eventually Rob was back at it again for a third go-round as season 20 of Survivor was going to be another All Star season with a new twist being Heroes VS. Villains. The most popular and unpopular players would be thrown on two separate tribes and of course Rob was placed firmly on the villains tribe, which was a surprise to him when he hit the beach with the other 19 players on Day 1 as he asked sarcastically, "I'm a villain?" Showing that being a married man and a new father to a baby daughter hadn't dulled his edgy ways, Rob immediately dissed the heroes by putting down the women on their tribe by saying they were inferior to villain ladies athletically.

Once back at camp, Rob quickly formed friendships with Survivor Pearl Islands winner Sandra-Diaz Twine and Courtney Sipes who were two of the physically weakest individuals on the villains tribe. He also had a big fan in Ben "Coach" Wade who admitted he was in awe of being in Rob's presence. Watching all of this unfold in the background was ultimate villain Russell Hantz who would soon be on a collision course with Rob for control of the tribe. With the villains tribe dominating challenges in winning four of the first five events, the Rob-Russell feud was put on the backburner. However the arrival of a clue for the hidden immunity idol soon lit the fuse between the two as Russell scampered off into the jungle in an effort to find it and reprise the methods that had him dominate the previous Samoa season (which Rob and none of the other contestants saw by the time they made it out for heroes vs. villains). Russell was violating Rob's edict of not looking for the idol and he vowed that if anyone did in fact go searching for it, they would be marked for immediate eviction. Things soon came to a head one night when Russell approached Rob to find out where his mind was at. Rob quickly informed Russell that the tribe was annoyed that he went to look for the idol and that he was a marked man. Russell defiantly stated that he would continue to look for and than eventually find the idol. Rob quickly cuts off the conversation and leaves with a "good talk Russell" as a parting comment. He later states in a confessional that he was trying to make Russell more paranoid that he was already and it was clear that Rob believed he was in full control of the tribe which were backed up when he stated about his new rival "he's not playing with the amateurs anymore."

Things would soon get nasty the next day as Rob mocked Russell in telling him he better find the hidden idol. After Russell informs him that he doesn't have it, in a classic Boston Rob reaction, he snickers and tells him "its been real." The connotation of course is that was Rob telling Russell that he is next for having the audacity of crossing him in the first place. Of course Russell did in fact have the idol but he still faced seemingly insurmountable odds in his own tribe with only two allies on his side in Parvati Shallow and Danielle DiLorenzo as opposed to the rest of the tribe of six being firmly ready to take him down led by Rob.

After being informed that both tribes would be heading to TC two weeks into the game, Rob hatched a seemingly fool-proof plan where he and the other five who made up the anti-Russell faction would split their votes on Parvati and Russell in a method guaranteeing that one of them would be sent home, even if the idol was played. However in one of the biggest "dumb" moves in Survivor history, Tyson Apostle decides to change his vote at the last second to Parvati which disrupted the 3-3 strategy by now making it a 4-2 count in her direction. Russell of course gave his idol to Parvati and Tyson was sent home as Rob looked down with a quizzical look on his face.

Not being one to give up of course, Rob immediately went to work in trying to retry the Russell ouster and this time all five remaining alliance members would go in the Evil One's direction. By this time Russell was hell bent on booting Rob but he still faced a shortage in the numbers with no idol to protect him anymore. By this point things were falling apart on Rob's side as Russell successfully convinced Jerri Manthey to vote on his side and Coach Wade proceeded to throw his vote in Yates' direction due to his inner battle of not wanting to vote for either of the tribe behemoths. Thus Rob was sent home by a count of 4-3 as Russell claimed victory after round 1 of their duel. No doubt it was a stunning and at the same time stinging defeat for the always overconfident Rob who no doubt was dealt a big piece of humble pie.

The next time Rob and Russell would meet of course was at the heroes vs. villains reunion show and it was there where a classic piece of Survivor television was cemented. The discussion soon began with Probst talking about the Rob-Russell rivalry during heroes vs. villains, specifically their differing styles of play. Rob answered a question on how thought Russell doesn't play to win but only to get to the end of the game. Russell, in his always smug manner, than shoots back "have you ever won?" which than brings about the all-timer response by Rob when he says that he "would have no problem going back out there and kicking your ass all over the island." The crowd went wild as even Probst started to laugh to himself. Russell quickly accepted the challenge and tried to shake his hand to cement the deal which Rob refused to take due to the fact that "he was done shaking your hand."

The plan for Rob and Russell to duke it out was quickly put into place as Probst reportedly took the lead in championing their rematch. A new twist was to be added to their season which would be called Redemption Island where those who get voted off have a chance to get back into the game by winning a series of duels against other evicted players. No doubt it was easy to surmise that this new concept was put in place in order to keep Russell and Rob around for as long as possible in the event either was booted early but instead of starting each guy on the same tribe to have at it, they instead were placed on separate squads with the unspoken goal being to see who could get further along in the game and than go at each other one they reached the merge.

Unfortunately however, the duel never materialized as Russell was voted out first from his tribe and third overall as his Zapatera tribe wanted nothing to do with him and threw a challenge to oust him from the game. Russell would than go on to lose his one and only Redemption Island duel to Matthew Elrod which left Rob to carry the story the rest of the way.

As far as Rob was concerned, Redemption Island was going to be where he left it all out on the table as far as this being his last chance to finally get over the hump and take home the title. He quickly went to work in forming a tight bond with the young and impressionable Natalie Tenerelli and than brought in two other alliance members in Grant Matos and Ashley Underwood. After an early setback for his Ometepe tribe in losing the first two immunity challenges, Rob quickly went to work identifying threats and eliminating them. Elrod was target number 1 after he had the audacity to congratulate Zapatera after they won the second immunity challenge. Rob also zeroed in on the fact he was growing flirtatious with teammate Andrea Boehlke which surely brought back memories to how powerful a romantic relationship could be in the game. So Rob engineered his first blindside by dumping Elrod and it soon became apparent that he was running the show and that everyone else had better get on board or they were finished.

Next Rob ousted Kristina Kell who was looking like another threat after openly looking for the hidden immunity idol. It was also after Kell's ouster where Rob formed an interesting bond with Phillip Sheppard who was one of the biggest loose cannons in Survivor history. Knowing he would need as many people on his side as possible, Rob took Phillip under his wing and made him a loyal "soldier" which played well for the former U.S. government agent.

Another highlight was Rob adapting to the new hidden immunity idol rules as he successfully found the one at the Ometepe camp as he further solidified himself into a position of power. From that point on, it was a Survivor performance unlike anything that had ever been seen before from a dominance perspective. Rob successfully engineered the one-by-one elimination of the Zapatera tribe at the merge, while keeping his Ometepe teammates in line and preventing them from defecting to the other side. He also booted Elrod a second time when he got back into the game from Redemption Island, with the key being his ability to convince Boehlke to cast her vote toward her former crush as well. Rob also won immunity a number of times along the way as he retained his ability in that regard as well, with the ultimate being the last challenge victory that solidified his place in the finals.

Once Rob got the immunity necklace fastened around his neck after that last challenge, he instantly became emotional as he had achieved his dream of getting back to the finals of Survivor and of possibly finishing what he had started over 10 years and 4 seasons ago. He would bring the combustible Sheppard and the unflashy Tenerelli to the final three which further established him as the clear favorite to win. This time around, the final TC was a bit milder from what he endured in All Stars, despite some hurt feelings from Grant who Rob voted out at the final six when Andrea won an immunity challenge when she was going to be the one to go. Rob gave a tremendous performance at the final TC and his effort on Redemption Island was perfectly summed up by jury member David Murphy who called it the most dominant season ever for a Survivor player. Rob would go on to win the million dollars and the title of sole Survivor by an 8-1 count as he embraced Amber and his two daughters at the reunion show. The icing on the cake came when Russell praised Rob for "playing a great game" and offered his hand in congratulations for a job well done. Rob had climbed the hill and finally conquered what he had set out to do all those years ago and like a great football player who finally won a Super Bowl, cemented his legacy as one of the best players to ever set foot in the game.

ANALYSIS

In my opinion, Rob Mariano's performance on Redemption Island gained him the title of the best player who ever played the game. It also was the most complete and utterly dominant game that has ever been played as it should be put into a manuscript as far as being the guide on how to win Survivor. What was also interesting when it came to Rob was the fact that he successfully underwent a transformation in the eyes of the viewing public from one of the most despised players ever to one of the most beloved. It was truly a remarkable feat that was just as impressive as his victory on Redemption Island. Either way, Rob made himself a true legend of the game that future players will be judged against.

Going back a ways, its clear to me that Rob went through a maturation phase during his times on Survivor. During his Marquesas appearance, Rob was a big time arrogant jerk who had an extreme narcissistic attitude about himself. His blunt commentary and rude sarcastic remarks earned the ire of both his tribemates and those watching at home. His "Bawston" accent seemed more annoying as well. Hence his immediate expulsion once the merge hit was not surprising and Rob clearly had some work to do on his game if he ever were to compete for the million dollars.

Fast forward to All Stars and this was where Rob took off even further in the unlikeability department. Booting out Rob Cesternino was fun to watch as he was the more insufferable of the two in my opinion but that early backstab would set the stage for a truly rub-your-nose-in-crap game play that would earn him fierce reprisals at the finale. What he wound up doing to Lex and Kathy was just beyond dirty and was one of the worst acts of deceit in the show's history. The fact that Lex put his game on the line to help out who he considered a friend and than have it turned back on him immediately was truly disgusting on Rob's part. Yes you can say it's a game and all that which is fine. However that plays more in seasons where the players have no history with one another. Lex and Kathy both knew Rob well and considered him someone they were close with. To have Rob do that to them when they stuck their necks out to protect Amber was disgraceful and was the biggest low point in his four seasons on Survivor. In fact that was the moment that

Rob lost All Stars. He wasn't about to recover from that since both Lex and Kathy were well-liked and had a tremendous amount of respect from the other players. It was a million dollar boneheaded move on his part and it ruined everything that he had done to that point on All Stars. It also put him on a level as truly one of the most disliked players to that point in the show's history and I know from my own vantage point, I couldn't wait to see him booted off. Rob and Amber together became the main villains of the All Star season and it was appalling to me how the others that were still left in the game after the Lex incident didn't just band together and vote him out than and there. However it never happened which could speak to how well Rob was able to dodge and weave from that point on. And without a doubt, Rob played an awesome game in All Stars, the breaking of Lex's legs notwithstanding.

In actuality, Rob should have won the million dollars that season. Amber taking it all was an absolute joke and a clear example of how a bitter jury refused to give the money to the better player. This was something that would repeat itself with Rob's prime enemy Russell during his first season in Samoa when Natalie White took home the prize in a gutless move by the jury. Now if it seems like I am both praising and killing Rob for his performance on All Stars, its because I am. The Lex move was beyond dumb but the way he was able to navigate through the game while placing a huge target on his back due the growing relationship he had with Amber was impressive. Creating the fight between Rupert and Tom at the final five to upend a possible coup against him was genius and he always seemed to stay one step ahead of the threats against his game. He literally carried Amber to the finals and obviously saved her with his politicking to Lex. She was along for the ride and did nothing to deserve winning that game. Obviously Rob sort of won when she accepted his marriage proposal and he thus shared in the winnings once their union became official but no doubt he had to be thinking deep down that he was….for lack of a better term…Robbed! He knew that he should have been named the winner of All Stars based on game play alone but he also had to know that he failed in the social aspect of it which undermined him in the end. It was here where the transformation of Rob Mariano the player began.

When Rob came back for heroes vs. villains, it didn't appear like much had changed when things got started. Mocking the other tribe's physical abilities once they hit the beach on Day 1 was classic in-your-face Rob but things would soon change once they got back to camp. He formed an alliance with Tyson, Sandra, and Courtney which was interesting in that the latter two were some of the worst challenge players ever. Still Rob seemed in total control with Coach worshipping the ground he walked on and Jerri and he hitting it off like old times. However Russell was lurking in the background and clearly this new face made Rob very uncomfortable. As you all know none of the heroes vs. villains contestants knew who Russell was as the Samoa season was shown on TV at the same time the taping for their season was taking place. He was obviously on the villains side for a reason though and this likely made Rob doubly wary about what he was all about. I had said this many times over that I thought it was ridiculously unfair to have Russell in the heroes vs. villains season for that reason alone. Not having a book on another player's game was a major disadvantage for the rest of the villains tribe and I am fully confident that Russell would have been the first one voted off if they had seen the destruction he wrought in Samoa.

Still Rob and Russell were on a collision course and it was going to get ugly. Rob in my view actually underestimated Russell, no doubt with not having seen him play being a chief reason for this. His statement of Russell not playing with the amateurs anymore was a clear remark of overconfidence and when he snickered at him the next day in telling him that he was next, was another bad move in that it further emboldened the Evil One to oust him. However Rob did his part in coming up with the brilliant plan to split the votes to nail either Russell or his main squeeze Parvati and flush the idol.

Only Tyson was an idiot and fell for Russell's BS that he was going to go in the tiebreak. It was a seemingly foolproof plan that would have booted Russell right out of the game and given Rob the satisfaction of owning him but Tyson ruined everything. Even more infuriating of course was Coach's sudden waffling about not wanting to vote for either guy as he too fell for Russell's garbage. When Jerri defected to the other side, Rob was toast as Russell got him out of the game as Coach threw his vote to Courtney so as not to give it to either guy. Rob got up beyond steamed as he refused to hug Coach and called him a "little man." He didn't even make the jury and when combined with the fact that he lost his battle with Russell, likely fueled him like never before to get back for an unprecedented fourth time to right the previous wrongs. A funny thing happened throughout his duel with Russell however and that was the fact Rob was now being looked at as the god guy. With Russell being arguably the most despised player of all time, Rob was now seen as the lesser of the two evils and his behavior was much less in your face while in heroes vs. villains which further helped him change his appearance to the viewing public. Thus when Rob dissed Russell at the reunion show, he received a huge ovation from the crowd for standing up to the bully and supplying one of the best quotes ever.

Redemption Island was the saving grace for Rob as he was given one last chance to put things together and save his reputation as a great game player who really had changed his approach to the social aspect of it, which of course was Russell's fatal flaw and what separated the two in the end when discussing who was the better player. Rob was a monster on Redemption Island and he was never truly in trouble at any point throughout its run. The way he commandeered his tribe and had them loyally eating out of his hand was magical. He decision to bust up Matt and Andrea right away was genius and served notice to the rest of the tribe not to step out of line. He successfully altered his game to take into account the hidden immunity idols which he found and carried with him throughout as a "break glass in case of emergency" weapon. Ultimately though his work with Philip was out of this world. Phillip was a major head case in every sense of the word but Rob needed him as an ally in order to continue surrounding himself with numbers. He was able to earn the trust form the perpetually paranoid Phillip and once he got his loyalty, he used him for all his worth in telling him where to place his votes. He also latched on to Natalie who was young and who needed direction which Rob gave her. He nurtured her along the way as a big brother would to his sister and he fulfilled his promise to her from day 1 that he would stay by her side. In fact the only whiff of controversy that Rob underwent on Redemption Island was voting out Grant but by that time there was no one else to kick which left him no choice. Yes the jury was a little bit tough on him but nothing outrageous like we saw in All Stars. When David stood up and boosted for him by saying he had played the perfect game, millions of viewers nodded their head in approval. Rob did in fact play the perfect game which even humbled Russell to admit as much at the reunion show.

Clearly, the game of Survivor had impacted Rob's life more than any other contestant ever. He won a million dollars, he met his wife, he shared in another million dollars, and he eventually had a family with his Survivor bride. I cant think of anyone in any other reality show who literally had his whole life shaped the way it had with Rob on Survivor. In the end, Rob takes the role in my opinion as the very best to every play the game. Whether you loved him or hated him, Rob Mariano was a must watch contestant who will truly never be forgotten.

SANDRA DIAZ-TWINE

Survivor Seasons: Pearl Islands, Redemption Island

Titles: Pearl Islands, Redemption Island

Biggest Rival: Russell Hantz

Claim To Fame: Only two-time Survivor winner in history.

Sandra Diaz-Twine has done something in Survivor that no one else can claim. The diminutive military wife has the noted distinction of being the only two-time winner in the show's history, along with having the title of being the only contestant who never has been voted off who played more than once. No doubt Diaz-Twine is about as unlikely a person as you would expect to be the biggest winner in the storied history of Survivor and critics have long argued the notion that she was undeserving of both titles. The fact of the matter however is that she cashed two fat checks from the toughest reality show there is which speaks volumes about her game, no matter how many times Russell cries foul over the heroes vs. villains outcome.

When Sandra first came on shore during the opening scene of Pearl Islands, nothing about her stood out as a future two-time champion. She was small, older, and it appeared as though she had little in the way of athletic ability. However Sandra would quickly prove her worth to the tribe by speaking in her native Spanish tongue to the local villagers in an attempt to outfit her teammates with the best possible supplies they could use back at camp. In one of the first confessionals of that season, Johnny "Fairplay" Dalton praises her up and down for being able to speak for the tribe and take charge of what was a very chaotic start to the game.

Once back at camp, Sandra seemed to just blend in as there were much bigger personalities on the tribe such as Rupert Boneham in his first Survivor go-round and Dalton. Diaz-Twine however would not take a back seat to anyone as she soon revealed her fiery side in a loud exchange with Dalton after he made it a point to say how she was a weak swimmer. Taking immediate offense to being put out there as a weak player, Diaz-Twine let loose with an intense rebuke to Dalton's statement with lots of curses thrown in. Dalton went back at her as the screaming match intensified. At one point Sandra gets up from where she was sitting and proceeds to run up to Dalton screaming at the top of her lungs as she says bellows "I can get loud too" followed by another curse word. Clearly Sandra was not going to back down from anyone which would serve her well in the game.

As far as strategy was concerned, Sandra got in tight with Rupert as she eventually ended up in an alliance with him, Trish Dunn, Krista Hastie, and yes Dalton (before the fight). This kept her protected as Burton Roberts and Michelle Tesauro bit the dust for not being in with their group. Sandra also found herself in the spotlight when she was picked to go raid the Morgan tribe of one item after her Drake tribe won a reward challenge. No doubt this was a sticky situation to be put in as clearly the Morgan people would look at Sandra as the one who plundered them but she was unrepentant in what she had to do as expressed in a confessional. She settled on taking their tarp and headed on her way.

Despite the notion that Sandra was a background player who let others make the decisions, she was the one who changed the dynamic of the Drake tribe when she found out that Trish was pulling a coup on Rupert. Sandra took the info back to Rupert and Krista and with spare part Shawn Cohen's help, ousted Trish for her deception while at the same time outing Dalton for going along with it. Eventually the merge arrived and Sandra and the rest of the Drake's (including the returning Burton) convinced Morgan outcast Lillian Morris to switch sides and vote out their leader, attorney Andrew Savage. It was at this point where the game started to get out of hand starting at the final 8 as Jon finally achieved the ouster of Rupert with the help of Burton and the rest of the Morgan's. This put Sandra and Krista on the outside looking in. However ever resourceful, Sandra was able to constantly dodge herself out of trouble right through the end of the game as she made the finals with Morris as prime enemy Dalton went out in the final three vote. It was in the final TC where Diaz-Twine described her strategy which would be something she would fall back on during heroes vs. villains as well. Sandra's plan was to constantly be the one who would be the swing vote and once things started to break down at the merge on Pearl Islands, she became that vote in almost all of the remaining TC's. She also made it through the entire game without earning a single vote which spoke to how she always managed to keep herself out of the spotlight which no doubt takes some skill. In the end Sandra annihilated the final vote by a 6-1 count as she took home the title.

Once her Pearl Islands victory was in the bag, Sandra was quickly approached to come right back along with Rupert for Survivor All Stars. Unfortunately she wasn't able to attend due to health issues stemming from a bout with parasites. She was also in the running to be on Survivor Micronesia Fans VS. Favorites but she didn't make the cut. However Diaz-Twine eventually made her back to the game when she was picked for the heroes vs. villains roster and she was placed on the latter tribe on the sides were figured out. Despite being in your face at times while in Pearl Islands, Diaz-Twine was not one you would consider a villain. However she was planted on the tribe anyway which was much to her surprise once they all hit the beach. However she would quickly give ammunition to those who believed she belonged there due to the fact that during the first challenge just minutes into the game, Diaz-Twine proceeded to rip off the top of hero participant Jessica "Sugar" Kiper. Just by being out there however, Diaz-Twine had the chance to show that her earlier victory in Pearl Island was not a fluke.

Once back at the villains camp, Sandra repeated her strategy to get in tight with the majority alliance which would be made up of herself, Courtney Sipes, Rob Mariano, Jerri Manthey, Coach Wade, and Tyson Apostle. Sandra became especially close with Sipes and Mariano who would be her biggest boosters in the game. Things were going swimmingly at first as the villains won four of the first five immunity challenges but than the Rob/Russell showdown hit the fan and the result of which would determine Sandra's future well-being in the game. When Russell came out on top in eliminating both Tyson and Rob, it was clear that her and Courtney were the next to go as they were deemed the weakest members in the remaining tribe. When it came to challenges, Sandra no doubt came up on the short end of things going back to Pearl Islands. She would be the first volunteer to sit out challenges due to her shortcomings physically and this was pointed out by Russell as the game moved along. Sandra had no respect for Russell but she knew all too well that she had to stay out of his crosshairs in order to get herself to the all-important merge.

Her key moment in the game arrived when the villains lost two more immunity challenges right before the merge as things were falling apart without Rob's leadership. Sensing an opportunity, Sandra fabricated a story to Russell that Coach was targeting him after the humiliation of the Rob vote where he looked gutless for throwing his vote. Knowing that Russell was constantly worried about threats to his game, he bought what Sandra was saying and Coach met his fate. Thus with one more TC session to get to before the merge, it was another key moment in Sandra's existence in the game as she knew all too well that it was either her or Courtney who would be sent packing next with Russell in tight with Jerri, Parvati, and Danielle. Miraculously, her good friend Courtney was the one who was shipped out next as Sandra survived to make the merge.

The merge itself was always the most important stage of the game for Diaz-Twine in that this was the time where voting strategies shift from taking out the weakest player when the teams were in tribes, to now looking to kick out the more physical players who are threats to take individual immunity. Thus it was another opportunity for Sandra to sail a bit under the radar and to reprise her role as someone who could be the swing vote. Once she got to the merge this time around, Diaz-Twine made it her mission to convince the heroes not to trust Russell but no one over there seemed to want to listen. One by one the heroes started to meet their fate while Sandra did her best to make a move against Russell once and for all behind the scenes. After being rebuffed at every corner, she had no choice but to stick with the villains so as not to put the target on her back from Russell. It eventually got to the point however where Russell turned on his partner in crime, DiLorenzo, while Sandra stood by to jump into the void, albeit reluctantly. However she sailed right through to the final three with Russell and Parvati and she proceeded to give the same speech she spoke of in Pearl Islands about how she always was putting herself in the swing vote position. The heroes on the jury, particularly Rupert, expressed regret over not listening to her warnings about Russell, which seemed to solidify her advantage over the other two the longer the final TC went on. Once the votes were read at the reunion show, Diaz-Twine was revealed to be the first two-time winner of Survivor. The two million dollars she won during her two appearances were also a record for a female game show contestant in television history. Clearly the jury refused to reward the ultra strategist that was Russell who left them all with a bitter taste in their mouths. Russell was extremely displeased by the results and went on the attack during the reunion show about how Sandra was not deserving of the title. The back and forth between the two would continue on in subsequent media appearances over the next few weeks but Diaz-Twine was unapologetic for how she won the game on both occasions. The fact of the matter was that she had successfully achieved a goal twice over, whereas Russell was left searching for his first win.

ANALYSIS

When looking at Sandra's history in playing the game of Survivor, the results speak for themselves. Anyone who goes 2/2 in winning the toughest reality show in history, no doubt was doing something right no matter whether you agree with her strategy or not. The biggest issue that critics of Sandra seem to hang themselves on is the fact that she played the under the radar game which is a major scourge for Survivor fans in analyzing what a winner should look like. Not so much with Pearl Islands since even her biggest detractors couldn't say that Lillian Morris deserved the million dollars over her, but the heroes vs. villains results really ratcheted up the arguments that Russell or even Parvati was robbed. In the case of Russell, his unmatched strategic game ran circles around some of the most accomplished players in Survivor history, whereas Parvati won some immunity challenges while serving as co-conspirator to the Evil One. The argument of more than a few fans were that Sandra's strategy and game play in heroes vs. villains should not have resulted in her winning the million dollars yet again.

My view on this is pretty simple: it's a bunch of baloney. Whereas there were some instances in Survivor history where the winner was not deserving (looking at you Natalie White), in the case of Sandra, this was not the case in either instance. In just discussing the heroes vs. villains controversy, anyone who says that Sandra didn't deserve the million dollars are not seeing the big picture. Its stating the obvious that Sandra is not built for the physical part of the game. That much is clear to see. Chances of her ever winning an individual immunity challenge is as likely as seeing her plant a big wet one Russell's bald head. However given the fact that Sandra can't compete in winning the immunity necklace, the result of this is that her path to the finals is that much harder than it would be for an Ozzy or a Colby Donaldson Australia version, who used this avenue to get to the end of the game. Sandra didn't have that security blanket which put more pressure on her to make her way through the subsequent TC's.

Another aspect that her critics miss is the fact that Sandra was a much better strategist than people gave her credit for. She outed Trish in Pearl Islands and got her voted off which eliminated some of the pressure on her earlier in the game. She also dodged back and forth around the Burton-

Dalton alliance who kept flip flopping seemingly every time they went to TC after the merge. Than in heroes vs. villains, Sandra convinced Russell to dump Coach when the easy choice was to send her home. These were all big time moves that didn't get enough credit.

Also Sandra's knack for being the swing vote during both Pearl Islands and heroes vs. villains was something else that was overlooked. While keeping herself away from the spotlight, Sandra in the process made herself a voting free agent who could be used to oust anyone from the game. The results were there for all to see and those who criticize her are just not being accurate about her game.

Really what I guess I am saying is that Sandra deserves her place right up there with Boston Rob as the premier Survivor players ever. I would love to see her come back for another shot and go for the three-peat but either way she doesn't have to take a backseat to anyone when it comes to Survivor worthiness. In fact Russell is sitting in the seat squarely behind her on that ride.

RICHARD HATCH

Survivor Seasons (2): Borneo, All Stars

Survivor Titles: Borneo

Biggest Rival: Sue Hawk

Claim To Fame: Also appeared on Celebrity Apprentice.

Talk about writing the book on how to play Survivor. Whether you love him or hate him, there is no denying the fact that Richard Hatch penned the blueprint on how to play the game and it was the strategies and methods he invented while out there in Borneo on this way to the million dollars, that have lived on in some form or another in every subsequent Survivor season. From inventing the very first alliance, to refusing to allow personal feelings or friendships to get in the way of advancing in the game, Hatch's performance during Survivor's launch season was no doubt a major reason the show caught on in the first place. Being an openly gay man who pranced around naked all day also brought attention to Survivor and his massively cocky behavior was exemplified when on day 1 Hatch claimed he was already the winner. Ultimately Hatch went out and made it happen by earning the 4 votes needed to take home the prize in front of a record-setting audience watching from home. Whereas his encore performance in All Stars left a lot to be desired, the legacy of Richard Hatch when it comes to Survivor is firmly entrenched.

When his Pagong tribe first hit the beach during the first day of the rest of Survivor's life, Hatch immediately brought attention to himself by throwing a bit of a hissy fit while sitting up in a tree due to the fact that the tribe was doing a million different things instead of getting to work. Jeff Probst would go on to say later that there was a strong belief in the producers room that Hatch would be the first person voted off due to his outspoken nature. However with this being the inaugural edition of Survivor, the radar's weren't buzzing among the other tribe members when it came to identifying Hatch as someone who should immediately be sent home due to his abrasive nature. Little did everyone know that Hatch had a clear ace up his sleeve in the form of being an excellent fisherman who went out into the water on a daily basis and came back to shore with fish for everyone to eat. The fact he was providing food in an environment that was as harsh as anything these people had ever experienced made Hatch into an indispensable player which of course was part of the plan. That way he can still pop off and act like himself without worrying about reprisals since he was supplying the one comfort that everyone craved the most while out in the elements. It even got to the point where the Pagong tribe was able to look the other way when Hatch disrobed and strutted around the camp without apparel.

When it came down to game play however, Hatch also showed he was very capable when it came to challenges. Being a naturally big man, Hatch had natural strength to go along with agility which made him an asset in that respect. Combined with the fact he was still catching food everyday, Richard Hatch was the one guy in the entire game that was almost untouchable.

As things moved along, the strategist in him came to the forefront as Hatch invented the very first alliance voting system which of course is now a staple in every other Survivor season from that point on. He pulled in a four person group with Sue Hawk, Kelly Wigglesworth, and Rudy Boesch. From that point forward, the four of them remained loyal to one another and proceeded to vote out the remaining players in the game. This included picking off the opposing Tagi tribe one by one once the merge hit with both teams having five members left. Hatch knew that once the advantage was gained in tribal man power, it made it easy to than simply get rid of the remainder of the group which simplified things. By the time the Tagi's got wind of what was going on, their effort to get Hatch out of the game was all for naught. Once the alliance made it to the final four, Hatch leaned on trusted friend Boesch who vowed to stick with him to the end. Luckily for

Hatch, Wigglesworth gave in to the temptation and voted out Hawk which broke a 2-2 tie. She than won the next challenge and decided she had a better shot to go beat Hatch in the finals where surely the jury would have some choice words for him.

Choice words indeed, with Hawk having the most profound statement at the end when he labeled Hatch a snake and Kelly a rat. What likely won Hatch the game however in addition to the much better strategic game that he played over Kelly, was his tremendous performance in the front of the jury. Hatch was a great speaker who was eloquent with thoughts and he proceeded to give very expressive answers to the jury questions which surely had helped him some. Soon the votes were cast and after the first three ended up in a 3-3 tie, the final parchment was opened to reveal Hatch's name in big letters. He instantly grabbed his head in amazement over just winning a million dollars and from that point on, he would have the title of the very first winner of Survivor.

The follow up to this trail blazing win out in Borneo made him an easy choice to help fill out the rosters for the Survivor All Stars season. With seasoned players who learned by surely emulating what Hatch brought to the table 9 seasons ago standing in his way, the challenge this time was a bit more daunting. However in his usually smug manner, Hatch went out doing his usual act of strutting around naked while going out and catching fish for the tribe, while making it a point to show everyone that he was doing absolutely nothing else around camp. Be that as it may, the food bit was working once again as Hatch kept everyone full and in his mind made it impossible to vote him out. A battle with a small shark that latched onto his arm during one of those fishing trips further emboldened his feelings of worth in the tribe as he brought his attacker back to shore and made a meal out of him.

However this being All Stars, the target was on his back as far as being someone the rest of the group was beyond wary of due to his extreme strategic game. Also the notion of taking down the first ever Survivor champ was a goal spoken openly by fellow tribe member Shi-Ann Huang. After losing Jenna Morasca to a voluntary exit to be with her ailing mother, the remaining five of Hatch, Lex Van den Burg, Colby Donaldson, Huang, and Kathy Vavrick-O'Brien began to size one another up. After coming in last in the immunity challenge a few days later, it was on to TC. Donaldson immediately targeted Hatch who got wind of the plan. With Lex and Colby tight, Hatch knew Kathy and Shi-Ann were the ones he had to get on his side and he put his plan out to them in the way only he could. It appeared they were receptive to it as Hatch proclaimed in a confessional "how dare he" in response to Colby's attempts to get him out of the game. In the end though, the girls refused to buy into what Hatch was selling and he was sent home fifth overall by a 4-1count in votes. As he exited, Hatch gave a food dance and claimed that he was "bamboozled." A characteristically loud exit for the always scene stealing Hatch.

ANALYSIS

The quick exit in All Stars no doubt was a letdown for both Hatch and for the production since he was a big time draw whether you loved or hated him. However it was clear to me in watching that season unfold that Hatch went in way overconfident and got ousted for it as a result. He was no longer playing with raw players and he tried to play the same game he did in Borneo which wasn't about to work. Sure he was humbled by his performance there but it shouldn't take away from all that he brought along in the first place.

Again the concept of the Survivor alliance came from the man and his ability to find a niche that made him an asset to keep around camp, in his case the priceless ability to catch fish, were two tried and true methods for success on the show. His bombastic approach was certainly not but he also was the rare player who was given the million dollars after ticking everyone off along the way. These contributions to the game are what his legacy is made up of and surely he would have played again if not for some legal issues he unfortunately got tied up in.

The fact of the matter is that Richard Hatch helped make Survivor what it is today as one of the most successful programs in television history. His initial efforts in Borneo and his personality while doing so brought people to the tube to see what he and the game was all about and the victory he claimed that season had been paid over many times by the show due to the elevation in terms of positive reviews he helped it establish.

RUSSELL HANTZ: A.K.A. The Evil One

Survivor Seasons (3): Samoa, Heroes VS. Villains, Redemption Island

Biggest Rival: Boston Rob

Claim To Fame: Voted Player Of The Year by the fans after both Samoa and

Heroes VS. Villains.

Russell Hantz is not for the faint of heart. Quite possibly no player in

the long history of Survivor has been more despised and at the same time

respected than the squatty, hair impaired, radically intense Mr. Hantz. Both

Mark Burnett and Survivor fans couldn't get enough of the guy as he

unbelievably made it onto the show to compete three times in four seasons

and left a long trail of destruction and betrayals in his wake. Flat out Russell

revolutionized how to play the game of Survivor and he served as the perfect

boost to the show that brought viewers back after the show began to lag

some.

Hantz made his debut during season 19 Samoa and he quickly shot out

of the game as a guy who would do anything or say anything to scheme his

way through. He would quickly explain his approach to the game early on

that season as a sort of psychology experiment where he would create chaos

in camp in order to get people even further out of their comfort zone. Hantz would also explain that he was going to control the rest of the players and get into their heads so he can further alter their behavior. Lying was also part of the equation when he told his Foa Foa tribe within the first few days that he was a victim of Hurricane Katrina's flooding which was nothing but a bold face fib. Finally, he began the first of what would be a Russell Hantz strategy staple where he would pick out the two youngest and most attractive females on his tribe and promise to take them to the end of the game. One of those two ladies in Samoa was eventual winner Natalie White. Despite all of his plotting and scheming, Russell couldn't win challenges by himself which was proved by his Foa Foa tribe getting destroyed by their more cohesive Galu counterparts through the early stages of the game. In fact if not for Galu's leader Russell Swan having to leave the game due to medical issues, its likely that Foa Foa would have been picked off one-by-one once the tribes merged. However Russell was not going to go quietly as he also showed off phase two of his Survivor strategy which was to collect each and every hidden immunity idol that was available. This was the great equalizer for Hantz and the rest of the Foa Foa's, who would be down to only four members to Galu's 8 once they did in fact merge. It was also at this stage where Russell cemented his legacy as the clear player of the Samoa season.

It started off when the Foa Foa Foursome, as they would come to be known, somehow convinced the Galu tribe to vote out one of their own in the form of booting Erik Cardona. Be that as it may, Galu still had the 7-4 advantage in manpower as they soon realized how much influence Russell was having on the game. They would target him the very next TC which is when Hantz pulled out his hidden immunity idol and exclaimed "I'm not done playing yet" as the shocked the Galu tribe who looked on as Kelly Sharbaugh went home in the biggest highlight of the season to that point. It was than that the remaining Galu members began to panic and turn on one another and this is where Hantz came in yet again as he convinced Shannon "Shambo" Waters to join up with him in a side bar deal to go to the end of the game. Shambo bought it hook line and sinker and so the opening was there for Russell and the rest of the Foa Foa Foursome to finish off the Galu's. The only detour along the way in that venture was Bret Clouser winning a late immunity that forced Russell to vote off teammate Jaison Robinson. Hantz however personally took matters into his own hands when he beat Clouser in the last immunity challenge. This prevented Clouser from reaching the finals where he would have easily won due to his squeaky-clean reputation in the game and for the fact his former Galu teammates would make up the majority of the jury. However Hantz, White, and third wheel Mick Trimming were in the finals and it seemed like it was just a formality for The Evil One to claim the victory as he was clearly the most dominant player that season.

However this is where Russell's problems on Survivor came to the forefront and that was his complete absence of a social game. Throughout his run on Samoa, Hantz played with a ridiculously rough edge that had him quick to criticize and verbally rip apart opposing players. His seeming lack of respect for others in the game when addressing them verbally would quickly prove to overshadow the strategic brilliance that he brought to the table. This would bear itself out in the final TC vote as White took home the crown in a big time upset by a tally of 7-2 as Hantz sat there visibly steaming over the result which he spent a large chunk of the reunion show railing against.

After getting only 10 days off, Hantz was immediately back at it again as a last minute inclusion to the Heroes VS. Villains season. The caveat was that none of the other 19 contestants would have been able to see Russell's Samoa season since it would be airing at the same time the heroes vs. villains season was taking place. No doubt a major advantage to have since he probably would be the first person voted out if the other veterans saw all the chaos he had caused in Samoa, Russell went right back to work doing what had worked so well the first time around. The much slimmer Hantz immediately zeroed in on Danielle DiLorenzo and Parvati Shallow as his two new young hottie alliance members as he once again looked to create firm footing for himself in the volatile villains tribe. He also spoke right off the bat of once again controlling the minds of his tribe mates just as he had done before. One early way he went about this in the first few days was to intentionally hide the villain tribe's machete and make it seem like old grumpy Randy Bailey had done it. His plan to create unrest and paranoia once again worked to perfection as Bailey was blamed and than subsequently voted out the first time the villains went to TC.

Overall though the villains tribe was rolling as they won four of the first five immunity challenges. This cut down some on the need for Russell to scheme and plot constantly but the seeds were being firmly planted in this time period regarding his rivalry with fellow villain Boston Rob. No doubt both men had outsized ego's that made their clash inevitable but Russell once again pulled a rabbit out of his hat in turning back Rob's challenge and ultimately got him voted out. He was helped by finding yet another hidden immunity idol which earned the ire from Rob in the first place but Russell was still down in numbers as the majority of the tribe was still after him. Knowing that Rob and the rest of his alliance would split their votes 3-3 on him and Parvati, Russell decided ahead of time to give the idol to her and take his chances in convincing Tyson to vote for Parvati as well to break the tie in feeding on his paranoia not to get voted out. Tyson was clearly ripe for the taking as he was not totally sold on the 3-3 split vote as he surmised (which was later backed up by Russell) that he was going to be getting the votes from the Evil Alliance. Not wanting to chance himself going home if things went awry, Tyson cast his vote for Parvati, who wound up getting the idol from Russell (thus wiping out the 4 votes to her name). This proved to be fatal for Tyson who got the three votes from the Evil Alliance and was sent home as he ruined Boston Rob's plan in crazy fashion as Russell sat there smirking. It was classic Russell as he once again skirted Survivor death and in the process he shook the foundation of Rob's alliance who started to crumble under his leadership.

The next time the villains went to TC, Russell successfully capitalized on the turmoil in the Rob alliance and convinced Jerri Manthey to vote with him and the other two ladies. Knowing things would still end in a 4-4 tie in that scenario, Russell than concentrated on currying favor with the always unstable Coach by showing him yet another hidden immunity idol that he had found. He showed it to him under the guise that he stick with him and that they will go far in the game together. Not wanting to turn his back on Rob and ruin his word, Coach was caught in a dilemma where he of course committed his all-time blunder of throwing his vote in a harmless direction which opened the door for Rob to be voted out by a 4-3 tally. Russell had won the penultimate duel with Boston Rob as he continued to show that he was not going to be stopped by even the highest-caliber of players.

On and on it went as the game progressed as Russell of course unbelievably had a hidden immunity idol handed right to him from the opposing heroes tribe by JT Thomas, who were under the guise that there was an all-girl alliance dominating things and who were going to vote him out next. Russell immediately turned it around and voted out Thomas at the first merger TC and proceeded to take out Amanda Kimmel next. He would continue to plot and scheme on the fly as he got rid of DiLorenzo who was showing signs of mistrust and replaced her more firmly by promising Manthey he would take her to the end of the game. After going to town on Rupert in a vicious verbal attack, he took him out next, followed by Colby Donaldson, and than officially backstabbed Manthey to get back to his second straight finals. A chance to finally right the wrongs of losing the previous season's crown.

In the end, the same bugaboo that torpedoed Russell's chances of winning Samoa ruined him in heroes vs. villains as the jury absolutely went to town on him in very biting terms. Pretty much every jury member who got up in front of Russell tore him apart and he stupidly went back at DiLorenzo in committing a huge Survivor sin by being an argumentative finalist when talking to the jury. He would receive not a single vote as Sandra Diaz-Twine took home her second Survivor million dollar prize as he was once again left fuming and ranting and raving during the reunion show. Emboldening Russell even more was the fact that for the second time in his two seasons, he won the $100,000 fan vote for player of the season which he used as a crutch to explain that he was really the champion in the people's eyes. It was also during the reunion show where Boston Rob publicly challenged him to a rematch which he quickly accepted.

For the third time in four seasons, Russell found himself back in Survivor competition as he and Rob would have at it again. They would be placed on separate tribes to start things off as Russell quickly gave a speech to his new teammates that he was there to help this time and that he was not out to screw anyone so to speak. His Zapatera tribe mates were instantly leery of him however, with the best exclamation coming from Mike Chisel when he said "oh no.....Oh No!"......when Russell first got off the chopper to reveal himself to the rest of the group. Despite this, Russell once again went back to the well in bringing in two young, pretty female alliance members in the form of Krista Klump and Stephanie Valencia. In particular, Russell promised Valencia that she was his number 1 trusted ally and that he would lead her to the end of the game. While all this was going on, the rest of Zapatera kept close watch in knowing that Russell was up to no good. Despite being up to his old tricks, Russell was not going to find the hidden immunity idol this time as it was discovered on day 1 by Ralph Kiser of all people. Be that as it may, he kept right on looking as Zapatera won the first two immunity challenges which kept strategizing to a minimum at camp. However a reward challenge would quickly change the sense of complacency at Zapatera due to Russell going back to his old deceptive ways when it came to the hidden immunity idol. After Zapatera captured the reward challenge, which came with a basket full of goodies, Russell correctly surmised that a clue for the idol would be in the basket. Sure enough he spotted it and with a sleight of hand, moved it into his pocket in one fell swoop. Mike however saw this and immediately told the others as Russell scurried into the jungle with Krista and Stephanie to read it. Mike and Ralph proceeded to follow Russell and confront him over his selfish move. Russell was caught red-handed and tried his best to explain that it was part of the game which only infuriated Ralph even more. The exchange ended with a just as intense Russell telling Ralph he didn't like the way he was coming at him, with the latter calling him "big boy' as he walked away. Once back at camp, Ralph and the rest of the non-Russell alliance Zapatera members decided to ultimately throw the next immunity challenge so that they could vote him out of the game and restore order. They did just that which became obvious to Russell who knew he needed to pull another miracle to stay in the game. He needed just one more Zapatera member to come over to his side in order to combat the split 3-3 vote that was sure to come his way, along with either Krista or Stephanie. He zeroed in on Julie Wolfe who seemed like she would be receptive since she openly exclaimed that she was in the game to win the money for her children. Julie seemed to like what she was hearing from Russell so the Evil One once again was smug in going to tribal council. Ultimately however, Julie decided to go against him as Russell and Stephanie each received three votes along with Ralph. A re-vote was done and this time Russell was voted out for the first time in three seasons. As he exited, he turned back in classic Russell fashion and said "I'll be back. Be ready." He than headed to Redemption Island where a duel with Matthew Elrod awaited. Russell was confident he would defeat Elrod who he actually seemed to take a liking to while they were together at Redemption. Despite a valiant try though, Russell went down against Matt as he faced an eviction that was incredibly early and disappointing. As Probst began talking to Russell about what happened, the Evil One showed a soft side as he began to cry into his buff. He admitted later that he felt he let down Probst and the producers due to the fact his duel with Rob was so hyped and that he failed to keep up his end of things. However despite the tears, Russell quickly shot back into form as he began to rail at Ralph who came to witness the event and than reported the Zapatera secrets to the Ometepe tribe. It was classic Russell as he went out on his terms. Afterwards he confessed that this would be the last time he would play Survivor.

ANALYSIS:

All right well the first thing I have to say is that Russell Hantz was hands down the Survivor player I hated more than anyone else by a mile. I was ecstatic that he came back for Redemption Island for the fact that it gave me another chance to finally see him voted out of the game which surely was the draw for many millions of viewers. However on the flip side, I will say that Russell was one of the very best, albeit flawed, players in the history of the show. He brought a strategy into the game that was classically brilliant from his domination of the hidden immunity idols to his ability to constantly get into the heads of opposing players and force them to do what he wished. He was phenomenal throughout but the big negative which continued to be his downfall was his complete lack of a social game. Russell has gone on and on about how he was the deserving winner of both Samoa and Redemption Island and on strategy alone there is no debate. However there is more to winning Survivor than just strategy and so his in-your-face style leaves a lot of damage in its wake from deposed players. This brings an overwhelming sense of revenge on the jury members' part when it comes time for the final TC. That's the biggest reason why he failed to win either one of his first two seasons and nothing less. He can say that he was the best but in actuality he played a flawed game in that he never made the adjustments that he needed to do to finally win. You only have to look at what Rob Mariano did in the Redemption Island season where he played the greatest game ever on Survivor to see how one can successfully change their approach for the better. Rob was probably the most despised player in Survivor history before Russell came along as he played the harshest game I ever saw to that point in All Stars. It took Russell's even more hated arrival to make Rob look like a saint in comparison and when the two butted head on Heroes VS. Villains, the latter came out smelling like roses who the fans openly rooted for. As much as Russell would hate to admit it, Rob proved himself to be the better overall player by still playing with an edge during Redemption but minus the arrogance he had shown before. I thought it was very big of Russell to congratulate him during the Redemption reunion show as he was completely housed in their duel and there was no escaping that fact. He ate a major dose of humble pie and it had to be tough for him to watch Rob run off with the win. Basically what happened to Russell in Redemption is exactly what would have happened during Heroes VS. Villains if the rest of the bunch had seen his Samoa season. That's why its going to be almost impossible for Russell to ever play the game again unless its another Heroes VS. Villains format where he could team up with someone like a Rob Cesternino who no doubt would have no problem teaming up with him in an ultimate evil alliance. I do think we will see Russell again because he likes the game so much but he has a ton of work to do to finally get himself over the top and win that elusive Survivor prize.

CHAPTER 2: JUST A CUT BELOW THE TOP

JERRI MANTHEY: SURVIVOR'S "BLACK WIDOW"

Survivor Seasons: Australia, All Stars, Heroes VS. Villains

Biggest Rival: Colby Donaldson

Claim to Fame: Posed for Playboy soon after Australia wrapped.

Perhaps no Survivor player has been more unfairly labeled over the years than everyone's favorite villainess, three-time vet Jerri Manthey. Being dubbed the Survivor "black widow", Manthey has carried a reputation, unfairly in my mind, of a nasty, impossible to get along with, intolerable Survivor human being. No doubt the dye seemingly was cast way back in her inaugural season in Australia, when a series of confrontations with the chef who couldn't cook rice, Keith Famie, drew widespread attention both in the game and in the social media world watching on television. Despite proving herself to be a very hard worker around camp, along with being a strong female performer in challenges, Manthey quickly became the one member on each Survivor tribe in its long history, who every other member of the group rolled their eyes about when in his or her presence. This led to Manthey being voted out before the rest of the Kucha clan after her Ogakor tribe got the manpower advantage right after the merge. Led by Colby Donaldson and eventual champion Tina Wesson, the argument went that Manthey didn't deserve to go to the end of the game over Roger Bingham or Elisabeth Filarski, so they all agreed to bounce her out which no doubt left some nasty revenge desires coursing through her veins as she made her exit.

Hence Manthey came back in All Stars wanting to prove her worth again, as old "friend" Colby wore a look of "oh great" when she sauntered out of the jungle on day 1 as the three tribes found out who else was playing the game. Manthey was put in a tribe with Ethan Zohn, Rupert Boneham, Wesson, Jenna Lewis, and Rudy Boesch and just like in Australia, she right away got into it with a teammate, this time Boneham over various things around camp. Eventually the two had it out over how to build the best shelter for a reward challenge, with Boneham eventually winning his argument about digging into the sand in creating a floor and benches. A Noah's Ark-type rain the night after they bombed the challenge with their awful shelter, put Manthey on near-voluntary exit status as she shivered in tears during the storm. Eventually though the tribe was divided up to the fellow Mogo Mogo and Chapera tribes (after Manthey got her quick revenge by voting out Wesson on day 3) and she ended up with Donaldson once again. With clear revenge on her mind, Manthey pioneered a plan to dump her old crush, which made her 2/2 in getting back at those who perpetrated her exit in Australia. During this time, she struck up a seemingly tight friendship with Lex Van Den Burg as the two agreed to watch each other's backs. Than after the Mogo Mogo's took on Boston Rob's main squeeze and old Manthey friend Amber Brkitch, Lex accepted a plea from Mariano to save her and that he would repay him later. This forced Lex to turn his back on Manthey who was beyond hurt at the betrayal when he went up and told her what was going on. So for the second time in two seasons, Manthey was ousted during the middle portion of the game after trusting in people she thought would go to the end of the game with her.

Her last chance at finding some sort of Survivor glory came in heroes vs. villains as part of the.....what else.....villains tribe as he brought along a black cowboy hat for the occasion. This time around, Manthey seemed to make it a point to keep her mouth shut and let the rest of the villains tribe eat each other up which is exactly what happened, led by the war between Boston Rob and Russell Hantz. Eventually Manthey was presented with a crossroads moment in the game when she had to decide between casting her lot with Rob or with Russell in a vote that could go either way. After originally voting with Rob and finding themselves losing the battle to Russell after some voting snafus, Manthey decided to jump ship and go with The Evil One. She would become a trusted ally of Russell who eventually cast aside original alliance member Danielle DiLorenzo in favor of her. Manthey was cruising to the end of the game as she took part in yet another vote to oust Donaldson, who she defeated in the final five immunity challenge to win her very first necklace. She had made the final four and needed to get by only one more TC to reach her first finals ever where she actually stood a decent chance of winning. However thinking he had a better shot in beating eventual winner Sandra Diaz-Twine, Hantz backstabbed Manthey after promising to take her to the finals, and she was sent packing so painfully close to the Survivor goal line.

No doubt the sense of regret and what could have been was on the mind of Manthey as she took that walk as the last person voted out of heroes vs. villains. However she played an excellent game and almost got rewarded for it. She had successfully adapted her approach the third time around and quite possibly in the process started to dispel the notion that she was this some sort of Survivor villainess.

ANALYSIS

All right I got a lot to say about Manthey and after reading this you are probably going to think I am the President of her fan club which is not the case but hear me out on this. Like I hinted at earlier, the notion that Jerri Manthey was some sort of queen bee Survivor bitch was way overblown in my book and was totally unfair to her. Yes she was edgy and had a quick temper but lets take a look back at the confrontations she had in the game and I bet you will start to see her in a bit of a different light. First of all when going back to Australia, Manthey had some big runs-ins with Famie that made her seem overbearing. However Famie proved to be very difficult to get along with himself as none other than Donaldson ripped him a new one toward the end of the game for blowing too much rice. Looking back on it, Famie was more trouble than was Manthey but his ability to do well in challenges made him into more of an asset for the tribe to keep around.

Now in looking back at All Stars, Manthey was totally justified in getting into it with Boneham who had a downright horrible idea with the shelter challenge and they paid a big price the night those rains arrived. Boneham screwed up royally which almost cost him the game and Manthey was absolutely right in challenging him on the awful plan. She than moved on from it and made what she thought was a solid alliance with the previously solid Van Den Burg, only to be backstabbed in the process. Sure she spoke openly about wanting revenge on Wesson and Donaldson which was a bit childish but overall she was nothing but a hard competitor during the series.

Finally, Manthey played her best and cleanest game in heroes vs. villains as she stayed under the radar in a tribe full of big time personalities and made a big move during the middle of the game in siding with Hantz who didn't burn her in the past like Rob did in sort of orchestrating her removal with the Van Den Burg deal. That move got her to the final four where she became the latest Russell victim of deception but she still won her first immunity necklace which was impressive in beating Donaldson in a close duel. Also if she had made the finals, with say Hantz and Sandra, its likely she wins the game since we know Russell was not going to get any votes, and for the fact that the jury would likely reward her for a solid game along with the realization she had never won before. It was right there for her only to be snatched up at the last instant. Still you had to give her credit for the effort and again I think her reputation as a she-devil is nonsense. I do think Survivor should move on from her and not have a Jerri Manthey 4 but ultimately she was proved herself as one of the most polarizing figures the show has ever had who made her presence felt while out there. Just ask Donaldson if you don't think so.

RUPERT BONEHAM

Survivor Seasons: Pearl Islands, All Stars, Heroes VS. Villains

Biggest Rival: Russell Hantz

Claim To Fame: Perpetual wearing of the hippie shirt along with having the pirate persona exemplified by the Pearl Islands setting.

No doubt one of the most beloved players in Survivor history, Rupert Boneham, was a character not seen on the show until his debut in the Pearl Islands season. The backstory about the Pearl Islands location was that it was a region where piracy was rampant and some of the best buccaneers traveled through the region plundering ships for gold and wealth. Than we were introduced to Rupert who had the gravelly voice that sounded like it came right out of Black Beard's mouth. He instantly earned approval from the audience based on his appearance and good natured persona. Taking things a step further, Rupert lived up to the pirate characteristics as he stole the opposing Morgan tribes shoes and sneakers which were laying out in the open next to where the he and the Drake tribe were sitting on day 1.

Once they got back to camp, Rupert again proved his worth by being one of the hardest workers to ever appear on the show. From dawn to dusk, Rupert was working on the shelter or going out to catch fish, which he did with a Richard Hatch-like efficiency. He also had tremendous natural strength which made him an asset in challenges as well. In fact Rupert would show just how strong he was when he won a reward challenge where he had to hold up a teammate who was suspended out over the water in a mano-a-mano duel against the younger and much more chiseled Osten from the Morgan tribe. Unfortunately, Rupert was lacking in the strategic game which caused him to get picked off soon after the tribes merged.

The popularity that ensconced Rupert during his stay on Pearl Islands quickly earned him an invite back for the very next season which was the All Stars campaign. Like his first time out, Rupert became an asset around camp while using his strength to help out in the challenges. He survived an early scare when his tribe was decimated after losing the first two immunity duels but he quickly found his footing on the Chapera tribe in making an alliance with Boston Rob, Amber, and Jenna Lewis. The four of them rode it all the way to the end of the game where Lewis backstabbed Rupert in order to take the sure thing final 3 appearance. It was a bitter loss for Rupert who was so close to winning the million dollars as he surely would have done due to his popularity. However he was given a lifeline in the form of a fan vote for another million dollars to be awarded during the All Stars reunion show. Rupert wound up receiving an astounding 85% of the vote which netted him the cool million dollars that he came so close to winning months earlier.

Finally Rupert came back one more time for heroes vs. villains which was an experience quite unlike the other two due to the intensity of the game. He would fracture his toe in the first minutes of the game during a reward duel and than see his heroes tribe on their heels after losing four of the first five challenges. However Rupert made sure to get into a firm five person alliance with Amanda Kimmel, JT Thomas, James Clement, and Cirie Fields. Rupert would go on to the final six which was his second straight very good Survivor performance off his earlier than expected ouster from Pearl Islands. However he grew openly disgusted with the play of Russell Hantz and he called him on it in front of the remaining tribe. Russell than proceeded to tear Rupert apart as he mocked him over his good guy label. It was a downright vicious attack which left Rupert sitting there shaking his head. He would soon be voted out on Day 36. So close but still yet so far from that coveted Survivor crown.

ANALYSIS

Rupert quite possibly is my favorite all-time Survivor player and no doubt he is on the same list for millions of more fans of the show. He had that cuddly teddy bear persona that instantly drew you in and for as big as he was, he was a softie at heart like when he began crying after his pet lizard past away during All Stars. However he was also fiery in nature when he was crossed as Johnny Fairplay found out after he tried to oust him in a failed attempt during Pearl Islands. Rupert gave it all he had during his attempts at winning Survivor and he came agonizingly close during All Stars and Heroes vs. Villains. Unfortunately he was never able to get over the top which no doubt leaves him unfulfilled in that regard.

The biggest issue I had with Rupert and what surely kept him from taking home a Survivor title was the fact that he severely lacked in the strategic part of the game. Whereas guys like Boston Rob or Russell Hantz used unending strategy to get to the end of the game, Rupert never was tuned into that aspect of it. Other than entering into some alliances, he never took the initiative when it came to looking ahead in the game. His lack of smart strategy was even more pronounced during Heroes vs. Villains when he failed to take heed of the warnings that Sandra was supplying to him about how devious Russell was and how he should be taken out. Rupert thought this was a ploy on Sandra's part which of course it wasn't. His lack of trusting his former Pearl Islands teammate ruined his shot at winning the million dollars which he expressed for when he spoke to Sandra at the final TC.

Rupert was also too trusting in his alliances which also caused him to make some poor decisions along the way. He trusted in Lewis too much in All Stars when it was clear she was thinking of jumping ship to Rob and Amber which she ultimately did. Rupert should have jumped on her first and prevented this from happening. Also in Heroes vs. Villains, Rupert stubbornly joined in with voting out Tom Westman, despite his alliance partner James sustaining a severe knee injury prior to the TC. It was an incredibly poor decision, especially since the heroes were reeling from dropping their fourth challenge in five tries.

It was instances like this that undermined Rupert's chance for finally staking his claim to a Survivor victory. As endearing and entertaining as he was, his lack of some of the core Survivor game plays skills prevented him from being recognized as one of the very best players to play the game while also leaving a big hole in his resume.

ROB CESTERNINO

Survivor Seasons: Amazon, All Stars

Biggest Rival: Rob Mariano

Claim To Fame: Labeled best player never to have won Survivor.

We were first introduced to Rob Cesternino during the Amazon season as the geeky kid from Long Island, New York who came in as a self-professed Survivor "expert." Knowing that he lacked in the physical aspect of the game, Rob C. (as he later became known in All Stars) used his extreme smarts and cunning ability to turn the Amazon game on its head. Strategically speaking, Cesternino used the art of lying as his Survivor weapon to advance in the game and the web of lies and deceit that he wrought during his stay in the Amazon was masked by an outwardly goofy and good-humored nature. Be that as it may, Cesternino cut more deals than a car salesman and flipped alliances more than any player who came before him to make the final three, where he was voted out right before the finale as Jenna Morasca went on to win it all. In defeat however, Cesternino came out of it as the clear star of the season which got him a quick invite back for All Stars a year later.

The All Star season itself was going to be a tough one for Rob going in due to the fact that his strategy of backstabbing and lying against unsuspecting cast members was going to be almost impossible to duplicate with his more experienced opposition. The element of surprise was no longer in play which meant a somewhat different strategy would have to be put into place. He ended up on the Chapera tribe with another all-time devious player in Boston Rob, along with Tom Buchanan, Alicia Callaway, Amber Brkitch, and Sue Hawk. Cesternino proceeded to lay back a bit and let the game come to him at first since he most likely figured the others were looking at him with a wary eye. Along the way it seemed like he was having a tough time fitting in with the group, as Callaway castigated him for not helping out enough during an early reward challenge where they had to design the best looking camp. Still Cesternino soon made his first big move in talking alliance with Boston Rob who was receptive to what he had to offer. Boston Rob offered him his hand in confirming the deal and so it was looking like Cesternino was once again getting himself into a strong early position in the game. What Cesternino didn't know however was that he was being duped and Boston Rob quickly cast him aside in the subsequent tribal council. Cesternino was as visibly upset as anyone who was ever evicted from the game during that particular TC as he slammed his hands down on his knees after the clinching vote was announced. Ultimately he was taken down by the same backstabbing method that he so expertly rode to the end of the Amazon season and he would correctly surmise during the finale that he was a victim of his past success. No one trusted him and so he was pretty much done before the game even started. You live by the sword, you die by the sword.

ANALYSIS

First off, I was shocked that Rob C. was not included in the Heroes vs. Villains season. Couldn't you just see him pairing up with Russell and running roughshod over the game? And really ever since All Stars, we have not seen or heard much from Rob as far as possibly being involved in playing Survivor anymore. This is just conjecture but I am thinking that his bad showing in All Stars gave the producers pause in thinking that maybe he was not going to be able to be effective at the game anymore since his backstabbing style can only play well on new players. However he surely would have been right with his peers in Heroes vs. Villains but it didn't happen for some reason.

Anyway as far as Cesternino's place in Survivor lore, there is no doubt he was deserving of winning Amazon. In fact he would have won if he got through that last challenge as Probst polled the jury during the reunion show about that possibility, with the majority saying they would have voted for him to win it. It was incredibly impressive to me the way he was able to get through the all male/all female portion of the game since he admittedly was not much in the way of a physical specimen compared to some of the other men on his team. Also as despicable as some may think, Rob's use of lying and alliance flip flopping was a thing of mastery in that he always stayed one step ahead of everyone else while doing it with a smile on his face. He more than lived up to his self-proclaimed Survivor expert opinion as evidenced by his play.

All Stars however was clearly a case, as Rob himself said, of being a victim of his past success. The Amazon season was not that much earlier than All Stars, so Rob's habit of lying and backstabbing was still fresh in the memories of the rest of the Survivor alumni. It was just like when Russell was booted out right away in Redemption Island now that others had a chance to see him play. Its out of respect for the ability they had to take over the game and so Rob should take comfort in that, as disappointing as it was that he was voted out so early. By the way it was great television watching his reactions as the votes were read with his names on it during his ouster in All Stars. The way he mouthed the f-word and how he slammed his hands on his lap when he was officially ousted. You could just see the hurt and shock on his face as he handed his torch to Probst. Classic stuff.

Anyways here is hoping that we haven't seen the last of Rob Cesternino. As much as I disliked him during Amazon and as much as I took delight in seeing him get a taste of his own medicine in All Stars, its right about time to get him back into the game. The last few seasons have lacked strategic players of Rob's ability and so now would be the best time to get him back out there.

COLBY DONALDSON

Survivor Seasons: Australia, All Stars, Heroes VS. Villains

Biggest Rival: Jerri Manthey

Claim To Fame: Now the host of the target shooting reality show Top Shot.

Colby Donaldson grew old with Survivor. How else to explain the steep drop-off in his performance from dominating Australia to having Amanda Kimmel say he was bad at challenges in Heroes vs. Villains. It was quite the steep decline for one of the most popular players of all time and surely it wasn't the storybook ending many expected when Donaldson came back that third time to finally try to claim the title many feel he deserved from Australia. As with all of us however, you cant escape the effects of time and Colby was the biggest Survivor example of this.

Of course no one would had even thought of such a thing after watching the 26-year old Donaldson burst onto the scene in Australia with his tanned bulging biceps and Texas good looks winning millions of female hearts while at the same time winning scores of immunity challenges (5 in a row at one point) on the way to the finals. It was downright impossible to not like the guy who worked tirelessly around camp, while also showing a tremendously competitive side accompanied by the charming smile. He instantly drew the attraction of Survivor's "Black Widow" Jerri Manthey and formed a tight friendship with the motherly Tina Wesson. Donaldson would reveal just how much he valued friendships and loyalty during the game by making one of the most second-guessed decisions in the history of the show. A decision that ultimately cost him a million dollars and left him searching for that elusive title.

I of course am referring to Donaldson's choice of picking Wesson to go to the final two with him over chef Keith Famie who drew criticism and won few fans during his run on the show. Famie got into numerous arguments with jury member Manthey and did next to nothing when it came to challenges and making relationships. It would have been a slam dunk clean sweep victory for Donaldson as his name would have been written in stone on the million dollar check if he picked Famie to go with him to the final two. Still he fought the decision internally due to the fact he felt Famie didn't deserve to be sitting in the finals, while Wesson did. In the end he picked Wesson and dropped the final decision by a painfully close 4-3 margin. Donaldson got up and cheered loudly when Wesson was made the official winner but you had to think he was surely second-guessing his decision at that moment.

Colby would soon get a second chance during All Stars, where he played with a much more noticeable edge. He winced noticeably when he saw that Manthey was also involved in All Stars when the tribes were introduced to one another and he instantly became moody while back at camp with his Mogo Mogo teammates. In particular, Donaldson had issues with both Richard Hatch and Shi-Ann Huang. After helping to oust Hatch, Donaldson would soon be given the boot which was led by Huang and Manthey who would come over to the tribe in the first twist of the game. No doubt Manthey was outwardly ecstatic about getting her revenge on Donaldson, who she felt backstabbed her in Australia after they seemed to have formed a bond early on. It was a disappointing outing for Donaldson who admitted afterwards that he didn't play well and he blamed it on not being 100 percent into going back out there to play again at the time the season took place. Getting back to his edgy demeanor, it was certainly very obvious that he was much more surly this time around. From berating Huang about how she was doing nothing in the game, to openly dissing on Hatch, Donaldson seemed nothing like the gregarious, sometimes bubbly personality that he was in Australia for whatever reason.

Donaldson would get one last chance to right his earlier wrongs when the cast for Heroes vs. Villains was gathered and he of course was placed on the heroes tribe. Unlike with the All Stars season, Colby was back to being the nice guy in Heroes vs. Villains. However his game got off to an embarrassing start when he was hog tied by Coach Wade who literally dragged him to the villains side of the beach during the opening reward challenge. Manthey of course was standing right there enjoying every minute of it as she continued to harbor ill feelings toward Donaldson. Still he quickly became a popular player around camp, with this time drawing the attraction of Sugar Kiper, which Colby quickly rebuffed.

The heroes tribe was getting decimated in ridiculous fashion as they dropped four of the first five challenges which caused tempers to flare. Colby went at it with James during the second TC as the latter berated the soon-to-be ousted Stephenie LaGrossa. Donaldson also found himself clearly out of the dominant tribal alliance made up of Amanda, Cirie, Rupert, James, and JT. He was on his own with Tom Westman and after the LaGrossa ouster, the two of them were lined up to be next, with neither being able to do anything about it except scramble for any sort of miracle.

Colby would get his first of a few stays of Survivor execution at this point as he and Tom successfully convinced JT to join them in dumping Cirie. Than after Westman was voted out, Donaldson benefited from James' knee injury to once again avoid what was a certain eviction. Clearly not wanted by his own tribe, Colby was truly on his own during this season but he was making the best of it. However some troubling signs would soon emerge regarding his performances in the challenges once the merge hit.

Unlike his time in Australia, where it looked like Colby was unbeatable in immunity challenges, ten years later he was a shell of his former self. In fact before his ouster, Colby wound up finishing well behind the already injured James during a challenge where each tribe competed for an individual immunity necklace. This was nothing like the guy who ran circles around everyone out in Australia. And things would only get worse as he failed to win a single individual challenge, with the lowlight being Kimmel saying that "Colby is bad at challenges." Say what? Colby? Sad to say but she was right during that season as clearly something was missing there. Age related? That would be the easy answer but it was tough to watch in any event

Eventually, he made it to the final five as Russell had other fish to fry along the way before he turned to the unthreatening Donaldson. He gave it a good go in the final immunity challenge before losing to Manthey, which was fitting since she proceeded to help vote him out for the second game in a row. Clearly this was not the way Colby wanted to go out in his Survivor career and even though he made the final five, it was looked at as a very underwhelming performance with regards to his game play.

ANALYSIS

Colby has certainly ran the gamut from a dominating player in Australia to a guy who was seemingly over the hill in Survivor years by the time Heroes vs. Villains came around. No doubt it was incredibly shocking to see the drop-off in his performance as far as challenges were concerned. In fact James summed it up the best during Heroes vs. Villains when he talked about how disappointed in how bad he looked, which was followed by his classic comment that he was now "Superman in a fat suit." In fact the only reason why Colby made it as far as he did that season was because of James' injury. If James doesn't hurt his knee, than Colby goes home at tribal council number 6. From that point on despite being given another chance, Colby did next to nothing as far as strategy and stepping up in challenges. In fact I was tremendously disappointed that he was continually allowing Russell to bully everyone around camp and do nothing about it. Like for instance during that epic Russell-Rupert confrontation late in the game. As Russell goes on a nasty attack against Rupert, Colby just sat right there and watched it all unfold without saying anything. Not one word. He should have stepped right up and defended Rupert, who doesn't need help anyway but just for the sake of doing what's right. This was not the same guy who verbally reprimanded

Keith for using too much rice in Australia in front of the remaining tribe. It was almost like he was intimidated by Russell.

Also it was disappointing the way Colby went off on his brother who was struggling during the family visit reward challenge. After not seeing his family, specifically his brother, for over a month, he proceeds to continually rip into him in a very nasty way. It was very uncomfortable to watch. I will chalk it up to brothers being brothers to a certain extent but still he should have been just happy to see him and not be so intense.

Now for the Australia bit. No doubt Colby's decision to bring Tina to the finals cost him a million dollars and is a top five all-time bad move in Survivor history. Whereas JT giving the idol to Russell was just plan dumb, Colby's decision, while meaning well, went against everything there was about how to win Survivor. Sure the show was only in its second season but anyone could have figured out that he was a sure thing victorif he took Keith to the final. It would have been a 7-0 tally easy. Of course I still think the jury got it wrong in picking Tina over Colby. The way Colby dominated in the immunity challenges should not have been used against him as it was with some of the jurors. Its incredibly tough and against tremendous odds to win that many individual challenges in a row and he should have been rewarded for it. No questions asked. Still the decision to go with Tina no doubt has kept him up at night a few times no matter what he says.

Overall, I think Colby Donaldson was one of the better players to ever take part in Survivor but he is clearly a step below from the elite such as prime enemy Boston Rob, Russell, Richard Hatch, Ozzy, and Sandra. Maybe he will see him again and he will have the chance to restore his Survivor name but until than, he remains a cut below the top of the heap.

OZZY LUSTH

Survivor Seasons: Cook Islands, Micronesia, South Pacific

Biggest Rival: Parvati Shallow

Claim To Fame: Briefly dated fellow Survivor contestant Amanda Kimmel

"The best immunity challenge player to ever step foot in Survivor." That would correctly be the title given to three-time veteran Ozzy Lusth who redefined dominance when the immunity necklace was at stake. Ozzy was as close to unbeatable as you could get when things got physical but for as great as he was in that arena, the flip side was that he came up woefully short in the strategic and people skill portions of the game which undermined his efforts along the way.

Things started off great for Ozzy however in Cook Islands as he used his tremendous natural abilities in swimming and agility to continuously win challenges for his Aitutaki tribe. Just when the team looked like they would run away with things, the tribal switch threw those plans by the wayside as Ozzy and the rest of the group began to scramble. Still once the merge hit, Ozzy became a man possessed in winning five of six individual immunity challenges as he made the final three. Here was where his lack of people skills and strategy hurt him however as many on the jury made it a point to paint him as a loner and as someone who didn't really get to know them. So just like with Colby Donaldson, Ozzy lost a crazy close final vote by a score of 5-4. So close but yet so far.

Not to be undeterred, Ozzy came right back for the special Survivor Micronesia: Fans VS. Favorites season and proceeded to right the wrongs from Cook Islands. This time around Ozzy made it a point to interact with his tribe mates, which soon brought him into a romance with Amanda Kimmel. Their relationship caught the attention of the rest of the tribe, with Cirie Fields claiming that Amanda would later give birth to "little Ozzlets."

Despite the obvious attraction he and Kimmel had for one another, Ozzy kept himself focused on the game as he quickly found the hidden immunity idol after being sent to Exile Island during Episode 4. Having the idol clearly put him in a position of power in the game and in a real stroke of genius, he proceeded to add a dummy idol into the place he found the real one in order to throw off the next person who went there looking for it.

However despite owning the idol, Ozzy shut his Survivor radar off for just long enough to allow Parvati Shallow to blindside him during episode 10. Not sensing that he was in any sort of trouble, Ozzy (and Kimmel for that matter) were utterly shocked as the votes were read. He also left his hidden immunity idol back at camp as he clearly had no clue what was coming at TC.

The backstabbing from Shallow cut right to Ozzy's soul as he was still steaming during the reunion show. He proceeded to lash out at her for selling out their friendship, while at the same time professing his love for Kimmel as they were still together at that time. Eventually he and Kimmel would part ways, while the relationship with Shallow became healed.

No doubt Ozzy was in need of some Survivor redemption and so he made for the perfect candidate to go on the second installment of Redemption Island along with Coach for one last chance to get it right. He would be assigned at random to the Savaii tribe, while Coach went over to Upolu. Right off the bat Ozzy showed that he hadn't lost his physical touch as he quickly defeated Coach in a one-on-one reward challenge. Things were off to a rousing start as Ozzy seamlessly fit right in with his new teammates. Knowing full well that this was his last chance to learn from his past mistakes socially and strategically, Ozzy quickly formed an alliance with Keith, Jim, Whitney, and Elyse. And for the second time in two seasons, he found the hidden immunity idol as well. It was all set up for a long run through the game. But there was a nerdy teammate who went by the name of "Cochran" who would prove to be Ozzy's biggest impediment to glory.

As the two tribes headed to what seemed like a merge, concern grew about how Upolu member Christine was running off victory after victory on

Redemption Island. Knowing that it would be dangerous for another Upolu member to get back into the game, Ozzy took what can be classified as one of the riskiest moves ever in giving his hidden idol to Cochran and volunteering to be voted out so as to go to Redemption to knock off Christine. The move paid off as Ozzy successfully defeated Christine and than immediately came back into the game as the merge was upon them.

Going into the merge, the tribes were even in numbers which made it seem like a 6-6 split was on tap for the upcoming tribal council. However unbelievably the Upolu's convinced Cochran to jump ship and vote out Keith, as Ozzy won immunity. With Cochran's defection, the Savaii were sent to Redemption Island one right after the other, starting with Ozzy. So after sticking his neck out to protect Cochran, Ozzy was royally backstabbed again as it seemed like history was repeating itself. However Redemption Island offered him one last hope of getting back into the game and he proceeded to show off those extreme challenge skills that made him famous in the first place. Ozzy would go on to defeat in order: Jim, Keith, Whitney, Dawn, Cochran, Edna, and Brandon to return to the game for the final five. Cochran and Edna in particular gave Ozzy a tough go of it but he looked like a guy who lost nothing as far as his ability to win challenges when the stakes are the highest.

Once back in the game, it was clear that the remaining four of Coach, Albert, Rick, and Sophie were all against Ozzy due to the fact they correctly surmised he would easily win it all if he made the finals. For Ozzy the task was simple on paper: win the last two immunity challenges and win a million dollars and that elusive Survivor title. He got halfway there in winning the first challenge, as Rick was sent home. However the final challenge would be an agonizing loss where Ozzy went out to a huge lead, only to see Sophie come back and nip him in the end as she finished the puzzle portion first. No doubt in that moment Ozzy knew he had lost and that night's TC confirmed it as he was sent home in fourth place. One step away from greatness.

ANALYSIS

First off its stating the obvious that the line forms behind Ozzy when it comes to the best challenge player ever. He was as dominant and clutch as can be in that avenue and that aspect along made him a star. I also think he got jobbed in Cook Islands but it was close enough to not quibble too much. Ozzy's big problem was the social game though as he apparently didn't connect with enough people while in Cook Islands which caused the jury to have second thoughts about awarding a million dollars to someone who they didn't even really know. He successfully worked on that part of his game in Micronesia but he got royally jobbed by Parvati which could have happened to anyone. Yeah you can say he should have been more queued in as far as the threats around him and maybe the romance with Amanda distracted him as well but Ozzy deserved a mulligan there.

His effort in South Pacific however was tremendous and I cant argue with anything he did in the game with the exception of his move to give the idol to Cochran and volunteer to go to Redemption Island. It all worked out but that could have been an all-time blunder right on the same level of JT giving the immunity idol to Russell. If he would have somehow lost to Christine, we would be talking about Ozzy in much different terms. Still it all ended up well for him and he couldn't do much of anything with the Cochran situation. The Redemption Island performance was right out of the Matthew Elrod book and elevated his status even more in Survivor lore due to how he performed when the stakes were incredibly high. Unfortunately he couldn't win them all when he got to the final four and was edged out by Sophie. He predictably got out to a big lead in the physical portion of the challenge but the puzzle stumped him as he proved he was no Boston Rob. Rob was the rare Survivor player who was great in both aspects of the challenges in using your physical and than mental skills. Ozzy was completely lost on the puzzle and that was it.

Despite the fact he never won the game, I would have no problem calling Ozzy one of the best players to ever play Survivor. He picked up his social game along the way to go with his awesome challenge skills and he was also very quotable and entertaining on camera. The storybook ending was there for him in South Pacific but Survivor is not one for going along with the script.

TOM WESTMAN

Survivor Seasons: Palau, Heroes VS. Villains

Survivor Titles: Palau

Biggest Rival:

Claim To Fame: Former NYC firefighter.

Score one for the old guy. Surely that had to be a random thought that went through the eyes of Survivor viewers as their got first glimpses of New York City firefighter Tom Westman. Coming into his Palau season at 40 years old, Westman served the role as the token older male player which is part of the demographic during every new Survivor season. However Westman would quickly prove to be your non-typical over 35 competitor as he showed off a physical capability that was typically seen in much younger players. No doubt his occupation as one of New York's finest helped keep him in top tip shape and so Westman was able to easily avoid the stereotype that other players have for those who come into the game with gray hair.

It was obvious that Westman was going to be able to hold up and even excel when it came to the challenges but he would also show a very good strategic game as well. Knowing that an alliance is always a key component of getting far in the game, Westman proceeded to solidify a four person pact with Ian Rosenberger, Katie Gallagher, and Stephenie LaGrossa. It was later revealed that this agreement was made before the tribes hit the beach as the group of 20 players were sequestered together before heading to shore. Once they all hit the beach, the tribe were chosen gym class style, with Westman, Rosenberger, and Gallagher all ending up on the Koror tribe. LaGrossa meanwhile ended up on the doomed Ulong tribe which of course made Survivor history by never winning a single challenge as a team. Instead of hanging out in the background of Koror, Westman moved to the forefront and took a leadership position. He had clearly earned the respect of the rest of the tribe and the results in the challenges spoke volumes. Strategically speaking, Westman also brought in two more alliance members in the form of Gregg Carey and the late Jenn Lyon.

As the game continued to be dominated by Koror, Westman took his contributions at camp to another level when he proceeded to catch a shark which of course would be a huge source of food for the already successful tribe. Eventually he would be reunited with LaGrossa who came over after the rest of her tribe was completely decimated to the point that she was the last member remaining. Westman pulled her back into the alliance and thus there was clear path to the end of the game in place.

Once things got down to the final 8 however, Westman began to see things start to unravel and the time to start scrambling had arrived. Gregg and Jenn formed a tight flirtatious bond and they soon decided that LaGrossa was a threat that needed to be ousted. They were ready to go along with the plan until Janu Tornell decided to quit. Westman meanwhile had argued to keep LaGrossa in the game as another alliance member. Little did he know though that LaGrossa was ready to make a big move of her own at his expense. She tried to bring all the remaining women together in order to oust Westman due to the fact that it was now widely assumed he would win the game easily if he got to the finals since he was dominating everything. Westman however got wind of the plan and than quickly counterattacked in kicking LaGrossa out of the game.

With that threat out of the way, Westman continued to excel in challenges as he won immunity to guarantee himself a final five spot. However things continued to get crazy as he soon discovered that Gregg and Jenn were planning to vote him out at the final five vote and they convinced Gallagher to go along with it. Once again in need of saving his own skin, Westman enlisted Rosenberger and Caryn Groedel to counter attack and beat Gregg to the punch which would result in a tie and a drawing of rocks. Rosenberger told Gallagher of the plan and, not wanting to take the chance of having her fate decided by rocks, went along with the effort to oust Gregg.

The final five brought even more drama as Rosenberger took Westman in a reward which he had promised to Gallagher. This in turn prompted Gallagher to approach Groedel and Lyon to form an all-girl pack to try and take down Westman again. It was getting to the point where Westman was being targeted by just about everyone but he showed how skillful he was in the strategy game by continuously getting himself out of trouble. After Gallagher and Rosenberger argued and made up over the reward snafu, they turned back to the security of their original alliance and voted out Groedel.

The Final Four saw Westman win yet another immunity challenge which was needed as he yet again was targeted by the others as they all knew full well that they had no chance to beat him in the finals. It was now Rosenberger's turn to try and form the plan to oust him before the challenge and Westman would go on to find out about it. This caused Westman to completely lose all trust in Rosenberger who was privately saying he was with Gallagher to the end of the game. The two of them would thus be forced to vote for Lyon, while Westman went the other way in voting for Rosenberger as a statement of how he was through playing with his ungrateful teammate. Rosenberger however beat Lyon in the fire making challenge and made the final three.

With Gallagher and Rosenberger clearly planning to work together to get Westman out of the game once and for all, the onus was on the fireman to win the last remaining challenge. Of course it was going to be endurance in nature in a test of who wanted the million dollars more. After Gallagher bowed out early, Rosenberger ultimately decided to take himself out of the challenge after 12 grueling hours in an act of apology to Westman for being deceitful to him during the game. Thus Westman won his fifth immunity challenge out of seven which tied the all time Survivor record with Colby Donaldson, Ozzy Lusth, and Terry Deitz from Panama. Knowing he had a slam dunk win if he went to the finals with Gallagher, Westman did what Colby should have done in Australia and proceeded to guarantee himself the million dollars which he did by ousting Rosenberger. In the end Westman took the title by a 6-1 tally. In the process of winning the dough, Westman proceeded to redefine the expectations for players who were a bit on the older side.

After a long absence from the game, Westman enlisted for another run during the Heroes vs. Villains campaign. Clearly trying to do better than his near perfect outing in Palau was going to be next to impossible, Westman nevertheless did his best to replicate his past success as best he could by quickly forming an alliance with heroes teammates Donaldson, JT Thomas, and LaGrossa as he put their rocky past behind them. He also once again proved an asset at camp as he helped corral some wild chickens who wandered into the camp.

Despite the positive start, Westman would quickly discover he was not in Palau anymore as the heroes dropped four of the first five challenges and seemed to live at TC. After being in agreement about Sugar Kiper being the first to go, Westman quickly found himself out of the majority as LaGrossa was sent home next. It became apparent that Thomas had abandoned his alliance with Westman and Donaldson and instead formed a new pact with Rupert Boneham, James Clement, Amanda Kimmel, and Cirie Fields. Now the target would be put squarely on he and Colby's backs and there was little that they could do about it.

Westman helped delay the seemingly inevitable by showing that he still had his knack for excelling in challenges by quickly winning a mano-a-mano duel against Russell Hantz in episode 3's immunity challenge. However the heroes dropped the next two after that bit of minimum success and Westman knew he would need a miracle to survive the vote. Luckily the tribe received a clue for the hidden immunity idol which they all instantly set out to find. Westman would ultimately find it but did a poor job of trying to stuff it in his pants without anyone seeing. Kimmel spotted it and instantly told the rest of the tribe. With his new piece of protection in his pocket, Westman went back to JT and tried to convince him of the smarts of ousting Fields in order to keep the tribe strong and give themselves the best chance of getting back into the game. JT bought in and decided to vote with he and Donaldson to oust Fields. Westman played the idol which was a good thing since he got three votes which were canceled out. Fields went home and he and Colby seemingly had a new lease on Survivor life.

Unfortunately it was only a temporary salve as Westman would find himself voted out the very next time out, even in favor of the freshly-injured Clement by a tally of 5-2. Going out in fifth place no doubt was a real bummer for Westman and for the game itself since was such a great player. Still he failed to hook on with the right alliance from the start and that sealed his fate. It was that simple.

ANALYSIS

Like with Rupert, Tom Westman is truly one of my favorite Survivor players of all time. The guy was a class act all the way and was the total package of being a prime challenge guy along with being sharp strategically. His run in Palau is right below Boston Rob's Redemption Island season and Russell Hantz' Samoa season as the best and most complete outings in

Survivor history. That season alone stamped Westman as one of the best overall players no matter how quickly he went out in Heroes vs. Villains. And in regards to Heroes vs. Villains, it really just came down to the fact that he didn't get in with the right people from the outset. Alliances were drawn up so quickly, that Westman was left out of the inner circle and no matter what he did around camp, he was not going to be able to overcome it. Of course the idiotic decision for the rest of the heroes to keep Clement in the game when he was already badly injured over Westman was a downright joke. Seeing him go out so early that season was beyond disappointing for me because Tom really was too good a player to go out that quick. We as fans were robbed from getting to see more of him and even though he had aged some since Palau, there is no doubt in my mind that he would have went a long way if given a proper chance to do so. The real shame is not seeing what could have been.

CHAPTER 3: WE WON'T SOON FORGET THEM

JOHN COCHRAN

Survivor Season (1): South Pacific

Biggest Rival: Jim Rice

Claim To Fame: The Second So-Called Survivor Expert After Rob

Cesternino

Quick what is "Cochran's" first name from Survivor South Pacific? Yeah I didn't think you knew it right off the top of your head without looking above and hence that was the instant attraction to the guy with the last name of the famous O.J. Simpson lawyer. It was during the opening scene of Survivor South Pacific where Cochran let it be known that he was a Survivor junky through and through and that he was there to put his stamp on the game. He showed his cockiness by asking Probst to be called by his last name of Cochran and from that point in, it was the label he went by around camp. In the preceding days and weeks, Cochran successfully established himself as a co-star of the season along with Ozzy Lusth due to his candid and thoughtful confessionals and for his dogged determination to show that pale, Harvard nerds could hack it out there in the elements of the game. In the end he more than held his own as Cochran forever stamped his place in Survivor lore.

As I stated earlier, Cochran did his best to put himself out there as a player as he knew all too well that skinny kids who look like they couldn't lift a log were instant targets for eviction due to the belief that they can't help enough with the physical demands around camp and especially during challenges. It also didn't help that the young, good-looking factions of the tribe quickly grew into a relationship which left Cochran even more out of the loop. However as he espoused on more than a few occasions, Cochran loved everything and anything about Survivor and so to be an early boot would be unthinkable. After Savaii lost the first two immunity challenges, it seemed like it was just a formality that Cochran would be exiled but much to his surprise and relief, the tribe looked to knock out Semhar Tadesse and Mark Caruso first. It was at this point where Cochran started to get his foothold on the game as he began talking strategy with fellow Survivor thinker Jim Rice. Rice was concerned about Ozzy being the power player of the tribe and his growing relationship with young hottie Elyse Umemoto caught their attention. Thus Cochran and Rice teamed up to oust her at the next tribal council as the two smart guys on the tribe started to impose their will, much to the delight of the saved Cochran. Savaii than ran off two wins in a row in the immunity challenge which further allowed Cochran to work on his relationships in the tribe, especially with alpha male Ozzy. As the tribe watched Upolu's Christine Shields dominate at Redemption Island, a plan was put into place where Ozzy gave up his hidden immunity idol to Cochran and volunteered his services to head to Redemption and knock off Christine which of course he did. The tribes than merged with 6 members apiece with a seemingly tie vote coming up at the first tribal council. However Upolu sensed the disrespect that the Savaii had for Cochran and they quickly seized on his vulnerabilities as they convinced him to join them in a plan to oust Keith. Feeling like he was going to be out at six with the Savaii tribe who never seemed to give him the time of day, Cochran went along with it.

After the Keith vote, the claws came out from the scorned Savaii as the remaining members took turns browbeating him. It got downright nasty as Whitney told Cochran that he made her sick, while Rice ripped badly for his betrayal. No doubt feeling some regret over the move, Cochran was in too deep to turn back. He helped the Upolu's vote out the rest of the Savaii tribe one-by-one and thus unbelievably found himself in the final seven. However like he feared, the Upolu's didn't allow him to go any further as they stayed true to one another and made the statement with their voting out of Cochran that they really used him to get the other tribe ousted. He than headed over to Redemption Island where a matchup with Ozzy awaited in a possible seminal moment for him. This was Cochran's opportunity to take down a challenge legend. On paper this was a gross mismatch but once the challenge commenced, Cochran gave Ozzy a huge scare in coming within inches of knocking him off during a maze-themed duel that centered on guiding a ball through the course to the finish point. The upset was right there for the taking but he came up just short. A great effort nonetheless and even though he didn't win the game, Cochran no doubt made himself into a household name, for better or for worse.

ANALYSIS

You got to love Cochran. Before I get to his game play, there is something to be said for a guy going into Survivor with as big a physical disadvantage as you could have but who still went in with a bright smile and anticipation of doing good. One look at Cochran screamed "no way" as far as his ability to handle it out there in the always harsh Survivor environment but the guy's love for the game was incredibly palpable. No doubt he was an instant favorite for Mark Burnett and the rest of the production crew with his well-thought out responses to questions and his exuberance combined with ever present paranoia that made him almost a funny character to watch. It was like watching Rob Cesternino reincarnated. A guy who couldn't match up physically with the rest of the group but whose big time intelligence advantage helped even things up some. Clearly though, Cochran would have been road kill if the tribe didn't vote out Semhar or Mark instead. Cochran was a sitting duck at that point who was completely at the Savaii mercy. However given new life in the game, Cochran went to work and made it his effort to get himself strategically into the thick of it. The relationship with Rice had big potential since both were very intelligent and both had a very good mind for the game. In fact on a side note, I think Rice was a star in the making who could have done some big things in this game if not for Cochran's move to Upolu. Anyway the move to oust Elyse was Cochran's first big piece of Survivor attack but he soon lost his way with his conversion over to Upolu. The tie situation is always risky with the rock situation but it was a no-win scenario for Cochran in that he was going to absolutely burn all of his bridges from the Savaii clan who would be making up the majority of the jury if he made it to the end of the game. It was the wrong move and he ultimately was used by the Upolu and than discarded when they were done with him.

Looking back on his game, I am sure Cochran has some regrets but so does every other player who didn't win the game. What is not up for debate is the fact that Cochran had a real mind for the game and guys with his strategic skill set have been few and far between the last few seasons. I get the nagging suspicion that we haven't seen the last of Cochran and no doubt he will be once again be a must watch just like he was the first time around.

BEN "COACH" WADE

Survivor Seasons (3): Tocantins, Heroes VS. Villains, South Pacific

Biggest Rival: Russell Hantz

Claim to Fame: Wrote, directed, and starred in his own movie.

There may not be a more deep thinking, eclectic competitor in the

history of Survivor than one Benjamin "Coach" Wade. Blessed with talents

in many different disciplines, we were first introduced to him during Survivor

Tocantins where the Coach moniker stuck like glue due to his background

leading women's college soccer for 13 years. However Coach also revealed

his scholarly side while in Tocantins as he habitually quoted such historical

luminaries like King Arthur and Shakespeare, while spinning some wild tales

around the fire each night that elicited more than a few chuckles from his

disbelieving tribe mates. Coach also labeled himself as the tribal "dragon

slayer" who would take out those who stood in his way of winning the game.

Finally, he came up with nicknames for some of his other competitors, for

example calling his closest ally Tyson Apostol "assistant coach", eventual

winner JT Thomas "warrior", and runner up Stephen Fishbach "wizard."

Through it all, Coach proved himself a very capable competitor who wound

up going all the way to the final five where Thomas reneged on a promise to him and helped vote him out. Perhaps the highlight for Coach however came during the reunion show when it was revealed that he had in fact passed a lie detector test from the story he told about being captured by indigenous people while out on a solo expedition in the jungle.

It was a short time later where Coach came back out for Heroes vs. Villains, where he was placed on the villains squad for some reason or another. As odd as he might have seemed in Tocantins, Coach didn't give off the tone of a Survivor villain but he was placed on the tribe nonetheless as he vowed to "trust no one and slay everybody" on the way into the game. He quickly became smitten by being in the presence of Boston Rob as he outwardly genuflected to him on day 1. He also struck up a relationship with Jerry Manthey as the two flirted with one another and cuddled a bit at night. No doubt catching Manthey's eye was made much easier when he hogtied and literally dragged her arch-enemy Colby Donaldson during the opening reward challenge as he won his turn in dominating fashion.

Pretty soon the lines were drawn in the tribe between Boston Rob and Russell Hantz which left Coach in a very uncomfortable position as he had respect for both guys. Whereas Rob genuinely wanted to work with Coach in the game, Russell's plan was to play him and use him only as a means to win the duel. Russell went about earning Coach's trust by showing him the hidden immunity idol. Coach was impressed at how much of a hard core player he was and in an cringe-worthy moment, bowed down in front of Russell in a mock King Arthur scene. This would lead Coach to commit his biggest Survivor blunder ever when he chose to throw his vote in a harmless direction during the ultimate Rob/Russell TC showdown which was the difference in the former being sent home. As Rob gathered up his belongings, Coach tried to embrace him, which was quickly refused as he called him a "little man." No doubt that whole affair made Coach look gutless and he was soon sent out of the game during the very next TC with Russell leading the way for his eviction. It was a horrible ending for Coach in Heroes vs. Villains and he admitted during the reunion show that he was not happy how he was perceived and if given the chance to play again, he would abandon his dragon slayer bit.

Well that last chance to play Survivor came in the form of the South Pacific season as both he and Ozzy Lusth returned to find redemption and clear their names. For Coach, this was his moment to finally show that he could play the game correctly and show what needed to be done to finally win. He quickly showed that he was a different player when he pulled together a five person alliance on day 1 which included of all people, Russell Hantz' nephew Brandon Hantz which was not yet revealed at that point.

Coach also made a relationship with Edna Ma on the first day which kept him in the clear as far as imminent trouble was concerned. One person who did make Coach nervous was Christine Shields who claimed in the first few minutes of the game that she would put a big target on his back. Well in his best Boston Rob eliminate your threats right off the bat moment, Coach proceeded to get her voted out along with her closest ally Stacey Powell. With that threat minimized, Coach continued to lead the way as Upolu seemed to be a team of harmony, unlike the Savaii which had some upheaval going on.

Soon the merge beckoned which is where Coach once again showed that he had learned something along the way as far as how to adequately play the game. He and the rest of Upolu knew they had to infiltrate the Savaii and find their weak link in order to split up what was looking like a 6-6 split at the vote that night at TC. Coach quickly surmised correctly that John Cochran was that man and he proceeded to demonstrably state his case to him about how it was time to step up and not take the crap that Savaii had done to him throughout the game to that point. He literally drew a line in the sand and implored Cochran to cross it which of course he did. This allowed Coach and the rest of the Upolu to vote out the remaining Savaii, including Lusth, one by one and get to the end of the game six strong plus Cochran. All through that time, Coach strengthened his relationship with Brandon Hantz who revealed to him early on that he was in fact Russell's nephew. The news at first stunned Coach and made him very nervous knowing full well how he was made to look like a fool by his uncle. However for the betterment of the overall tribe, Coach went along with it and it all worked out in the end as Brandon remained loyal.

Eventually Coach and the rest of Upolu coldly kicked out Cochran and than Edna which left the original five alliance members in the game. Since Coach earned some more Survivor kudos by finding a hidden immunity idol, he was in firm control over how the end of the game took shape as he continued his Boston Rob Redemption Island performance. Brandon was let go next, who lost the final Redemption due to Ozzy which brought him back into the game. With Lusth quickly winning the next immunity challenge, the moment of truth was at hand for Coach to finish what he started and win the game. The choice was to vote out either trusted friend Rick, who really didn't do much of anything along the way Survivor-related to earn credibility for a win, or dump fellow alliance stalwart Sophie Clarke who already won two individual immunity challenges and had the well-spoken ability to do well in front of a jury. It was here where Coach first dropped the ball in voting out Rick who was beyond stung at the decision, and just like with Boston Rob in

Heroes vs. Villains, he refused to shake his hand as he left to get his torch snuffed.

Thus Clarke won the next challenge, sending Ozzy home and Coach was in the finals for the first time along with the unliked Albert Destrade. This was the chance that Coach had waited for but unfortunately the bridges he burned by those last few votes made him look bad in front of the jury and cost him the title by a 6-3 margin to Clarke.

ANALYSIS

Coach might very well be the most quirky and yet misunderstood player in Survivor history. As I said earlier, it was off base putting him on the villains tribe in heroes vs. villains as he was anything but. Yeah Coach was annoying at times with his antics and stories and he did some strange things, but he was nothing as far as nasty or unethical in his playing methods. Coach was just different which of course opens himself up to ridicule and mockery in a world where being outside the norm in behavior and character is considered a bad thing. The fact of the matter was that Coach really was kind at heart and no doubt was right up there with anyone who ever played the game as far as intelligence goes. This is a guy who conducts the Susanville

Symphony in California along with his many other ventures. And whoever can quote King Arthur religiously has some serious brain cells. Be that as it may, Coach's massive intelligence didn't translate well to Survivor as he became much too paranoid and distracted by things going on around him in the game, especially in his first two tries. Challenge-wise he was tremendous and always gave it his all. However strategically Coach was a mess and he admitted as much going into South Pacific. In Tocantins and Heroes vs. Villains, Coach was too much concerned about playing with "honor" and "integrity" which is basically Survivor death sentence words. Flat out you can't play this game by subscribing to either of those wishes. Lying must be done at some point and rough decisions need to be made which was something that Coach just couldn't bring himself to do. Ultimately this ruined his attempts to win his first two times out. It was impressive that he made it to the final five in Tocantins and much of that was due to solid friendships he had made with Tyson and JT. However in Heroes vs. Villains, he was completely out of his league with the villains tribes as the much bigger personalities there swallowed him up entirely. He started out all right as far as voting with Rob in the majority but he quickly fell for Russell's crap and that ultimately led him to do the Courtney throw away vote which was one of the most cowardly moves in Survivor history. As much of a Coach fan as I am, I have to call it like it is and say how ridiculous that vote was, especially in a game of that magnitude. He looked like a complete fool and he quickly realized he had been played as he was sent on his way by Russell the next TC. Just ugly.

South Pacific however changed many opinions about Coach as it should have. It was only to a certain extent however as I will explain. He did a masterful job in quickly forming that five-person alliance on day 1. Coach was finally taking the bull by the horns as far as protecting himself strategically and he also covered his bases with Edna and becoming friends with her in case one of the original five needed to be removed for whatever reason. He led the way in challenges and than had his finest moment in giving that awesome speech to Cochran that sealed the deal and convinced him to jump aboard to vote out the Savaii members from the game. It was all right there for Coach to win it all but he than blew it at the end when he voted out Brandon and than Rick over Sophie. The Brandon and Rick votes showed Coach to be a backstabber as he made promises to both guys. Especially in the case of Rick, who everyone liked as a nice, honest man, Coach looked terrible in doing what he did. Keeping Albert around was the right move obviously since no one liked him and this was shown in how he got zero votes at the final TC. However Clarke was a real threat that needed to be taken care of before it was too late and he failed to realize this. Probst

even confirmed how much Coach messed up at the reunion show when he

polled the jury by asking them if they would have given the title to Coach if

he took Rick to the finals. They raised their hands and confirmed that Coach

had the win in the bag. What a tough way to lose the game. No doubt that

decision is going to haunt Coach for quite awhile as he was that close from

having the storybook ending that he craved so much. Along the way though

he helped to erase some of the opinions about his game play from a strategic

point of view. He dropped the charade of the dragon slayer as he said he

would and he made it a point to play the game as hardcore as he could since

this would likely be the last time he would play it ever again. In the end he

failed but also at the same time he won.

CHAPTER 4: SURVIVOR CELEBRITY ALUMNI

Like with any reality show, if it goes on long enough, invariably a celebrity or two will pop up along the way and join in on the action. Through 23 seasons and counting of Survivor, they certainly have not been immune to having a famous person hit the beach in a quest for action and adventure, with the money being a consolation prize if they were to win. While you couldn't fill an 8 person tribe of past celebrity performers on Survivor, the few that have crossed over have no doubt been or turned out to be some of the biggest names in their respective industries. So let us take a quick look back on those individuals and how they held up during the game.

1. Elisabeth Hasselbeck (Filarski): Perhaps the most well-known Survivor contestant to ever play the game as far as mainstream pop culture is concerned, Hasselbeck made her debut in season 2 Australia where she was not yet married to former NFL quarterback Tim Hasselbeck, and where she also was not yet the famous co-host on the morning gabfest The View. Although very slight physically, Hasselbeck proved herself a very good and fit athlete who was also a big time positive presence around camp. She quickly developed a close relationship with Kucha elder statesman Roger Bingham, who would eventually take the hit for her and volunteer himself to be voted out so that the unknowing Hasselbeck could make the final four where she ultimately was voted out. Hasselbeck was also a routine crier while in the Outback and she also started to lose her hair toward the latter stages of the game due to malnourishment. After Survivor, the ultra-Conservative Hasselbeck made her way onto television via the Style Network on a program called "Style For Less" where she went about looking for fashionable clothing at a cheap price. She ultimately wound up on The View where she has been a stalwart co-host for the better part of 9 years.

As far as my opinion of Hasselbeck in Survivor terms, she was kind of just there in Australia despite making the final four. She never shined in any aspect of the game and was really a non-factor other than slipping by due to the fact Ogakor had bigger fish to fry before they got to her.

2. Jimmy Johnson: Those who are not tuned into both college and NFL football might not have known what all the fuss was about when Johnson ended up on Survivor Nicaragua at the age of 67, which fulfilled a lifelong dream for one of the show's biggest fans. Johnson of course was one of the most accomplished football coaches in history, winning both an NCAA championship with the Miami Hurricanes and than later two NFL Super Bowl titles with the Dallas Cowboys. Once Johnson retired from coaching, he became a regular studio host of the top NFL pregame show, Fox NFL Sunday. Part of Johnson's downtime was catching his favorite program Survivor and when he finally made the cut (after being rejected at the last second for failing his physical before Survivor Gabon), he was more than pumped about seeing how he could do in coaching up his new teammates. Unfortunately, the initial theme for Survivor Nicaragua was to divide the tribes according to age, with Johnson being placed on the over 40 bunch. This immediately put him into trouble as the older players weren't as awestruck in being around a famous television personality as the younger tribe would be. In particular, Johnson's teammate Marty Piombo seemed to not give a hoot about Johnson's fame and so after surviving the initial tribal council, and than winning his heat in the second immunity challenge which his tribe won overall, Johnson was sent packing on day 8. He admitted afterward that the experience was much harder than he thought it would be and that he was more miserable there than in any day in coaching.

In my opinion, Survivor Nicaragua went bust the day Johnson went out. The season itself was a complete train wreck but it was made worse when the drawing card that was Johnson left the show so soon. Piombo was the pioneer to get him out which is why I couldn't stand the guy but honestly

Johnson was in a bit over his head there. I also think Survivor did a disservice to him by having his season be the age split scenario. Johnson would have instantly won over the younger crowd and likely would have stayed longer if the tribes were made up with traditional demographics. I loved how he coached the tribe up during his stay and it was clear to see the power the guy had with words but unfortunately the show ended too soon for him.

3. Jean-Robert Bellande: Those who got caught up in the poker craze of the early 2000's no doubt knew who Bellande was. Extremely talkative and flamboyant at the poker table, Bellande was an interesting pick to join the Survivor ranks in order to see if his abilities to strategize and bluff while playing cards could possibly carry over to Survivor. In fact Bellande was not the first poker pro target of the show, as fellow top player Daniel Negreanu was contacted first but he refused to participate due to the fact he would miss the World Series of Poker. Bellande however quickly signed up and instantly became a draw during his Survivor China run as part of the Fei Long tribe. The husky Bellande actually did quite well in finishing eighth and serving as the second jury member. A continuing fight with Courtney Yates proved to be his undoing.

Overall Bellande didn't embarrass himself which is at most what you want to avoid as a celebrity participant. He didn't show off much of a lying or cunning game that we could relate to his poker playing and he seemed to annoy everyone at some point which is what he does at the table to get under opposing player's nerves and put them on tilt. However 8th place is nothing to sniff at and he cast his final vote for the ultimate winner, Todd Herzog.

4. Ashley Massaro: Joining Bellande as celebrity castaways in China was Massaro of WWE Divas fame. Blessed with big muscles to go with a smoking hot body, Massaro was a big time draw for the under-40 male demographic. However she quickly went bust on the show and was voted out after six days without much of a fight.

Massaro was a huge disappointment and it was shocking that a female participant who could bring it physically the way she could was not accepted by the tribe. No doubt if you gave her truth serum, she would tell you the whole thing was a big waste for her.

5. Gary Hogeboom: Former longtime NFL quarterback Hogeboom made his debut on Survivor Guatemala as he tired to make it a point to keep his identify secret by claiming he was the landscaper Gary Hawkins. The only problem was that eventual winner Danni Boatswain recognized him immediately as she was a former television sports reporter. It was later found out that the rest of the cast knew who he was but he was accepted nonetheless due to his friendly nature and ability to excel in challenges. He would eventually be voted out on Day 30 but Hogeboom etched his name in Survivor history by discovering and playing the first hidden immunity idol in the show's run.

I have to admit I didn't know who Hogeboom was and I am about as big an NFL fan as you could get. His playing days predominantly took place while I was still young which is the main reason I was not familiar with him but he also was not Joe Montana both in ability and notoriety. Still he proved himself to be a very good player who unfortunately was on the outside looking in from a big time alliance.

CHAPTER 5: THE HOST WITH THE MOST......JEFF PROBST

Survivor made Jeff Probst. And Survivor maintains because of Jeff Probst. Those two statements are not up for debate if one were to watch the entire run of Survivor like I have. When things got started way back when during that summer in Borneo, Probst was a previously unknown television personality whose life was about to change forever. Survivor would become an overnight hit and Probst would become the central character throughout. Over 20 seasons later, Probst is now one of the most recognizable personalities around and his iconic saying "The Tribe Has Spoken," has become a Pop Culture mainstay.

Of course it took Probst some time to get his feet wet and find his groove when it came to hosting this new phenomenon. If you were to go back and take a look at the Borneo season, you would be shocked at how…..lets see how I should put this….how boring Probst was as a host. It was completely like night and day to what he is now as the smooth talking, quick with a one-liner, beyond comfortable in his television skin front man for Survivor. However as the Borneo season unfolded, Probst looked nervous and unsteady in both his delivery and his mannerisms. His questions during tribal council were boring and lacked the edginess and the get-to-the-point inquiries that he has mastered over the years. Obviously that is no longer a concern and in my opinion Probst is the single biggest reason that Survivor is still as wildly successful as it is. The guy is an absolute star and has made the show his own. Probst is absolutely masterful in his handling of tribal councils as he always asked the questions that we as viewers are yelling at the television as we watch from home. He never stands for the BS that some contestants try to lobby toward him and he never allows a controversy to go by without a thorough discussion. On top of it all, Probst has developed a bit of intensity in his dealings with certain players during the game, with his obvious dislike for Johnny Fairplay during his run of antics in the Pearl Islands. He has immense respect for the show and will defend its sanctity to the very end. The fact that he continues to re-sign to host more seasons is beyond huge as I truly believe that the day he walks away from it, Survivor will die a quick death. He is such an institutional part of the show that it just wouldn't be the same without him. You can't tamper with perfection.

In the end I am sure Probst would even admit that Survivor made him into the star that he is now. Just for the fact that he was mentioned as a possible candidate to replace Regis Philbin of all people on Live With Regis and Kelly is all you need to know about how this show changed his life in ways he couldn't even possibly have imagined.

CHAPTER 6: THE HISTORY OF SURVIVOR GIMMICKS: THE GOOD, THE BAD, AND THE UGLY

One of the reasons Survivor has been such good television for so long is the fact that Mark Burnett and company have worked tirelessly to keep the game fresh by continuously introducing new concepts and ideas to change the looks of things. A program, especially when its of the reality variety, can quickly become stale if its allowed to remain in a status quo form. Survivor is not and has never been one of those programs however as they have routinely pushed these new mutations to the game from season to season. So without further delay, here is a quick trip down memory lane as I dig in and discuss which ideas worked and which ones should have stayed on the cutting room floor.

THE ONES THAT WORKED

1. FINAL 3 VERSUS FINAL TWO: For the first half of Survivor's history, the goal of each player was to make the final two as that would mean you had reached the last stage of the game and thus had a 50 percent chance

of walking away with a million dollars. Sometimes the vote would be very

close as it was for Borneo and Australia. Other times it would be a landslide

like in Palau. However starting with the Cook Islands season, three players

would now have the chance to stake their claim to the top prize which no

doubt changed things both from a game play and a viewing perspective.

As far as game play, no longer was it easy to just find the one person

who no one in the jury would like and than bring him or her to the final two.

With an extra person thrown in, a new element of complexity was introduced

to how the end of the game would be played. It was now much harder to plan

ahead in brining two different people to the finals as it was surely more

difficult to keep everyone in the threesome on the same page. Also from a

jury perspective, it gives them the chance to not be forced to vote for two

finalists who are widely disliked during their season such was the case in All

Stars with Rob and Amber.

From a viewing angle, I think going to the three person finale was

tremendous and it made things a bit more unpredictable when trying to

formulate in your brain who would likely be the winner. No doubt there was

zero drama in Palau when Tom Westman went to the end with Kelly

Gallagher. Or when Jenna Morasca went to the finals with Matthew Von

Ertfelda. As they say three's a crowd. Overall this was a big win in my book and it surely supplied a nice boost to Survivor as it entered some of its dog days after the high of All Stars.

2. REDEMPTION ISLAND: I have to admit that at first I thought Redemption Island was a horrible idea. The notion of having ANYONE come back into the game after being voted out was in my opinion going against everything that Survivor was all about. You get one chance to get to the end of the game and that's it. Once your torch is snuffed than say goodnight. My thoughts on this were cemented even more during the awful twist in Pearl Islands when Burton and Lillian were put back into the game after being voted out earlier. It was a downright ridiculous concept that season and when we didn't see a repeat of that fiasco from that point on, it was clear that the producers felt the same way.

Than Redemption Island was born during the Rob VS. Russell season. I will say that I thought once again that this was a terrible idea and it was obvious in my mind this was put in play as a ploy to keep Rob and Russell relevant for as long as possible. After hyping their duel so much, it would be a disaster if one or the other were ousted in the first few days. Hence the birth of the Redemption Island concept which was copied by one of the international versions of the show. That way even if Rob or Russell did get the boot early on, they would have a chance to get back in the game and thus not short circuit the entire storyline of the season before it had a chance to get going.

Anyways I decided to give it a chance in order to see what all the fuss was about. The first impression of it didn't sway me much as I thought it was an interruption to what was really important which was what was going on at camp. As impressive as it was seeing Matt Elrod make the run he did, it was a big yawner for me.

As things went on however, I had to admit I changed my mind. Once things started heading down the stretch, the duels took on major significance as Boston Rob was trying to go for his first ever Survivor title, while having to worry about Elrod coming back into camp and trying to take revenge for being booted twice. Also it turned out to be a real shame when Elrod wound up losing in the last challenge right before re-admission to the game which was something that stuck with me as well. Still even though I was coming around to it, I still was not completely sold.

However I firmly got on board the next season in South Pacific as Ozzy made Redemption Island his own. Along the way there were some truly nail biting duels such as Ozzy narrowly beating Jim, Cochran, Edna, and finally Brandon. Each one of those challenges carried quite a bit of drama and firmly thrust the concept into the winning column of good Survivor ideas. Sure its not ideal to have voted out players having the chance to return but the additional strategy that goes into it makes the game much more interesting.

3. TRIBAL SWAP: The concept of the tribal switch was introduced during season 3 (Africa) as a random half of the members of each team would have to head over to the other side no questions asked. This was a MAJOR alteration to the game as it destroyed alliances on the fly and forced the remaining players to adapt quickly to the new dynamics. It also proved to either elevate or destroy a player's stock depending on how they ended up with the switch. Boston Rob suffered tremendously from the tribal switch in Marquesas and soon found himself out of the game after looking like he was set up to dominate. No doubt it made things interesting and as far as the game was concerned, it forced the players to watch their behaviors even more than before since anyone in the game could be a teammate at any moment.

Some argue that, like in the case with Rob, the tribal switch unfairly undermines all of the hard work that was put in by some players early on in the game. While that may be true, the art of winning Survivor requires snap judgments and decisions due to things changing all around them. The tribal switch was just another example of this and it surely proved to be a success in my book.

4. Exile Island: The idea behind Exile Island was very shrewd in its thinking. Take a player out of the game entirely and drop him into an environment where its just them and nature. While on Exile, that individual has the opportunity to find a hidden immunity idol which of course guarantees a big time power position in the game. On the flip side, the exiled player is also missing out on what is going on back at camp. The rest of the tribe could be planning their ouster and so there is a major disadvantage in not knowing what is going on without you.

However there is a bit of a drawback to this concept and that's when an exiled player winds up finding the idol. If they don't wind up playing it right away, than the subsequent players who head there are searching in vain for an idol that doesn't exist there. Hence we are left watching someone looking through bushes and weeds with no anticipation of anything interesting happening. So it's a bit of a mixed bag. However the overall idea was a solid one and it added yet another way to throw the game on it's head a bit.

5. SURVIVOR ALL STARS: I absolutely love All Star seasons as do the fans based on the tremendous ratings for Season 10. We all love to see our old favorites come back again and this time have to do battle with one another in order to see who truly is the best of the best. It is a brilliant concept that every other reality show known to man was smart enough to adopt. The All Star season with Amber Mariano winning it all was a smashing success and left me wanting more. That's why I was doubly excited for Heroes vs. Villains which was basically All Stars 2 but with a fancy title. With Season 25 getting ready to debut very soon, here is hoping we get All Stars 3, whatever title they decide to give it.

6. Heroes VS. Villains: I know this can be considered sort of a subset of the All Stars format but the key idea was compiling the two tribes with who were considered "good" players and those who were considered "bad." What made this a successful concept was the fact that, primarily in terms of the villains tribe, those with a bad reputation in the game wouldn't get targeted right off the bat like what happened with Rob Cesternino in All Stars. The Russell's and Parvati's of the world would be forced to work with one another and the game itself would lose some predictability. It also was interesting to see how certain members of the heroes tribe went to the dark side along the way in their own setting. Coming out of that season looking worse than when they went in were James and JT as far as ethics were concerned. James was perpetually cranky and said some nasty things along the way, while JT channeled some of his inner villain by plotting and scheming like he was Russell. Ultimately this was a very good season that lived up to the hype. The one criticism which I have already espoused on though is the Russell situation of going into the game without the rest of the tribes seeing his season which was not right. Than again as much of a draw as Russell is, maybe that was a good thing according to the producers since if he was in fact exposed for all of what he did in Samoa, than he would have easily been the first one out and a major draw would have been sent to the sidelines.

7. FANS VS. FAVORTIES: This was another interesting concept that pitted newcomers against veterans. I liked the contrast to see if in fact those who studied the game at home and came in raw, could ultimately defeat their more seasoned counterparts. Ultimately the veterans came out on top with the much better schemers involved but it still was a new twist that allowed Mark Burnett to bring back some old favorites which is always a big draw for the show. Would have no problem seeing this done again.

8. THE HIDDEN IMMUNITY IDOL: Quite possibly no Survivor gimmick has had a bigger overall impact on the game and has had more staying power than the hidden immunity idol. First introduced during the Guatemala series, the hidden immunity idol took center stage during the Russell Hantz era as the man made it his mission to find each and every one of them during his three stints on the show. It even got to the point where people were giving it to him (you know what I am talking about). Anyways the beauty with the hidden immunity idol was how it was the main vehicle used to blindside an opposing player while at the same time, serving as an instrument for turning the game on its head when played correctly. Perhaps the greatest use of the idol was by Russell himself when he whipped it out during his Samoa stint to utterly shock the opposing Galu tribe who all cast their votes his way. Hantz used it to knock out Kelly and start the process of voting them out one by one as it completely turned the game around. Really the hidden immunity idol is the single biggest wild card in the game as it creates paranoia regarding who could have it, while also changing up voting strategy with the split vote becoming a new trend over the last few seasons. Sometimes it can get a bit much, like in Heroes VS. Villains when it seemed like a hidden immunity idol was played in every tribal council but overall it has done more to reinvigorate the game than anything else.

The hidden immunity idol has also served as the centerpiece of the biggest blunders in the history of the game and also have created ridicule to those who went out of the game without playing them. On the first note, we all know by now that JT did the stupidest thing ever on Survivor when he handed over his idol to Russell of all people during Heroes vs. Villains in thinking that an all-girl alliance over there was kicking out all the men.

Russell of course used it to vote JT out at the merge and sail into the finals. The one thing you can say in JT's defense though is not being given the opportunity to see Russell's season clouded his judgment some and that if he did see all of the destruction the guy wrought in Samoa, there is no way he would have done what he did. However JT had to know that Russell was not the cleanest player if he was placed on the villains tribe so he doesn't get too much of a pass.

Another awful use of the idol was during Micronesia when the famous ice cream scooper Erik stupidly gave up his idol to Natalie after being convinced that he was not going to be sent home. As soon as the necklace was around Natalie's neck however, Erik quickly met his fate as the girls continued to dominate that season unlike any other in Survivor history.

As far as those who got sent home without playing the idol, Micronesia was also where Ozzy packed his bags with the idol sitting in it. Topping that big time blunder however was James Clement keeping not one but TWO idols in his pocket as he got voted out in the final seven in China. As good players as these two guys were, they will always have these pock marks on their Survivor resumes.

Finally, the immunity idol has also seen itself morph into knockoff brands during the later seasons of Survivor and have been used in some classic "I fooled you" scenes ever witnessed at TC. I already referenced how Jamie Dugan of Survivor China got the wool pulled over her in playing an idol that was a dummy. However the best was during Survivor Gabon when the perpetually grumpy Randy Bailey played what he thought was a legitimate immunity idol that was created in very detailed fashion by that season's winner, 57 year old science teacher Bob Crowley. Bailey was completely set up and the look on his face was beyond priceless when Prosbt informed him that his "idol" was in fact a fake as the rest of the group snickered behind him and than proceeded to vote him out.

Obviously the hidden immunity idol is a keeper and the fact that it continues to throw the game upside down season after season is proof positive of why it's a keeper.

I HOPE TO NEVER SEE IT AGAIN

1. THE MEDALLION OF POWER: Quite simply the absolute worst Survivor gimmick was the laughably bad Medallion of Power which was introduced during the Nicaragua campaign. It went hand-in-hand with another theme that season which was the separation of the tribes by age, with one group being over 40 and the other being under 40. While the age split was interesting in a small dose, the Medallion of Power thing was a disgrace.

How it worked was that the tribe in possession of it would be given an advantage in the upcoming immunity challenge. During the early stages of Nicaragua, the Medallion was used on a few occasions which resulted in easy wins each time it was activated. The tribes were quickly scrambled after only a few TC's as the younger tribe started to dominate and the Medallion of Power was never seen again as well. This tells me two things: 1. The disparity of the tribes due to the age differences resulted in the kiddies running away with the game early which forced the producers to quickly switch things up so as not to continue with the landslide. The other thing it tells me is that the Medallion of Power went bust in both the game play and in general. The Medallion basically guaranteed victory for the tribe that used it which short-circuited the drama of the challenge. Mercifully, it was quickly shelved and we haven't seen it since. Lets hope is stays that way.

2. MEN VS. WOMEN: Boy do I hate the battle of the sexes. Originally started during Vanuatu and than repeated in the Amazon, the division of tribes into all female and all male demographics was something that on the surface looked promising but in the end was just a poor idea all the way around. It was funny when the guys dropped the first immunity challenge in Vanuatu but that was the one and only highlight in this gimmick. For starters, immunity challenges get destroyed because of this. In my opinion, the sanctity of the challenge is to blend raw athleticism and muscle from the men with the balance and agility of the women. When it's a men versus women situation, challenges can't be structured that way which makes them boring to watch. As an example, one of my favorite challenges over the years have been Quest For Fire where both tribes paddle from the water to the beach while lighting torches along with the strength challenge where the strongest guy on the tribe has to shoulder weight on a pole while the opposite team piles weight on it. You can't get these kinds of challenges when its men versus women.

On top of this, camp life is so much less interesting under this setup. There obviously wont be any flirting going on over at the sausage factory that is the men's tribe. The women on the other hand will usually sit around cooking and organizing which is not so much fun to watch either. It really takes away from the show. In addition, the makeup of alliances will be drawn up with all-males or all-females which is a drag as well. The best alliances of the past have almost always been made up of a mixture and they also have almost always formed early on in the game. All the way around this setup is ugly to watch and does nothing for the show. Unfortunately the upcoming Survivor Earth season is looking to be yet another example of this.

3. RACE SETUP WITH TRIBES: This was another disaster all the way around and it had nothing to do with the game play. For Survivor Cook

Islands, the players were divided into four tribes made up of each of the following races: white, black, Asian, and Hispanic. When I first found out about this, I instantly had an uncomfortable feeling. I felt a bit of embarrassment for Survivor due to my thoughts on that this setup made them look foolish. I don't know what they were trying to do in formulating the tribes like this. I mean were they trying to show which race was the best at Survivor? That one race was more capable of beating the other? Either way it was weird all the way around. Whenever race is involved with anything in life, it instantly draws wary eyes from the public and this was no different. This was a potentially combustible situation for Survivor in that they had no idea whether the tribes would put each other down based on their race in the heat of battle. They had to be worried about race being the talk of the game which could always blow up at a moment's notice. The word I keep coming back to is uncomfortable which is the best way to describe this season as a viewer. This was another setup that has been one and done and I truly think the higher-ups with the show look at that season as one that was experimental but in the end just didn't work. They are also lucky nothing controversial came out of this.

CHAPTER 7: THE HISTORY OF SURVIVOR ROMANCE

There is a popular saying that love can find you anywhere and pop up at anytime during your life. When it comes to Survivor, that statement can't be more accurate. Throughout the 20-plus season run of the show, there have been more than a few Survivor romances blossom on the shores of the various locations and some have even gone onto the ultimate step of sanctifying itself through the act of marriage. Survivor romance at its core is interesting due to the dynamics at play. For one, the two parties are complete strangers beforehand who are now thrust into as harsh an environment as you could possibly have millions of miles from home. Without basic necessities such as a toothbrush or a shower, their bodies quickly begin emanating some not so nice odors, along with that kicking breath. At the same time there is a grueling game going on of scheming, lying, and backstabbing in a quest for a million dollars. So how on earth can something develop between two smelly, lying, greedy people with the cameras rolling at all times? For all the reasons written above and more.

Just the fact of being on Survivor and away from your loved ones so long no doubt creates the situation where the castaways look toward one another for some sort of comfort and it doesn't even have to be of the romantic sort. Perhaps the most touching non-romance relationship was way back in Australia when good old Roger Bingham adopted the than Elisabeth Filarski as his Survivor daughter. These two had a big time bond while in the Outback and it got to the point where Roger volunteered to be voted out over Elisabeth due to the fact that she was younger and would need the money more than he did (that's a pretty funny comment in light of where Elisabeth is now in her life but it was touching nonetheless). Taking things beyond that realm, the romance part of it is along the same lines. Two people in need of some comfort and who are attracted to one another can quickly find something developing under the palm trees. And sometimes it may not even physically happen while out there in the game. On a few occasions these Survivor matches are cemented once the game is finished and everyone goes home. On the just completed South Pacific series, Whitney and Keith soon developed a relationship after being voted out of the show which began somewhat in Ponderosa and than blossomed even more when they got back to the States. Another nice example was the match made in heaven between the Survivor China virgin Erik Huffman and blonde bombshell Jaime Dugan. These two began flirting during the middle portions of the show but things never got a chance to get going after Dugan was voted out after unknowingly

playing a fake hidden immunity idol. Huffman and Dugan found each other

quickly after the show ended and were married soon thereafter.

In talking about marriage, the most famous Survivor family of course is

the Survivor All Stars courtship between Boston Rob and Amber Brkitch. We

all know the story there which I don't have to go over again but Boston Rob

was instantly smitten with her and the rest is history. They now have two

daughters together as Survivor's first family puts forth the next generation of

contestants.

Another obvious reason in regards to Survivor love happenings is the

fact that the contestants have always been populated by overly good-looking

people. Lets face it, more eyes will be drawn to the tube when there are hot

looking young men and women running up and down the beach in their

bathing suits and bikinis. Survivor capitalizes on this to a T as they almost

always have an eye on a contestants looks when it comes to putting the tribes

together. There are some exceptions of course but generally, eye candy is

everywhere once the tribes hit the beach. Putting all of these people together

in one place thus will lead to fireworks going off which is yet another draw

for television's sake. Reality romances are always a big deal, with the head-

scratching success of the Bachelor and Bachelorette being proof positive of this. So it makes sense for Mark Burnett and company to put the dynamics in place and see how things turn out.

Clearly, the history of romances on Survivor have been another aspect of the show that have become another part of its success. Viewers, women especially, embrace a good love story and its made even better when there are some lying and scheming going on at the same time. Only in Survivor can this situation be possible.

CHAPTER 8: SURVIVOR INJURIES-NOT FOR THE FAINT OF HEART

Survivor is a rough game. Anyone who has ever stepped foot into the game as a contestant almost always gives the same refrain when its all said and done. Physically and mentally it was the toughest thing they ever had to do. The physical part of course centers on the fact you have next to nothing in the way of food, while at the same time having to push your body to compete as hard as you can in the always tough immunity challenges. The chance of injury are thus very high in the game and throughout the years, we have seen this bore out in a sometimes gruesome manner. These injuries no doubt changed the course of the game in almost every instance and the individuals who suffered this form of Survivor fate no doubt would all agree that they would much rather be voted out by a blindside than to be removed from the game for a medical reason.

The first time we as viewers came to realize that Survivor wasn't all fun and games was during season 2 in Australia when of course Michael Skupin passed out into the fire after taking a mouthful of smoke while trying to get it started. As far as what we saw at home, things started with a very loud Skupin scream as the camera quickly panned to him running into the water in an effort to soak his badly burned hands. He continues to scream in agony as we got a shot of the skin absolutely peeling off all ten of his fingers as the rest of the Kucha tribe looks on helplessly. Skupin was immediately evacuated from the game and quickly taken to a hospital. The ramifications of his removal were astronomical due to the fact that at the time, Kucha had a firm 6-5 edge in manpower with one challenge to go before the merge. With Skupin proving to be their strongest and toughest player, Kucha most likely would have knocked off the reeling Ogakor clan once again and gone into the merge with a tremendous 6-4 edge and thus would be able to knock them off one by one. Instead they go in tied and than proceed to lose their advantage when Jeff Varner was sent home due to former teammate Kimmi Kappenberg having loose lips in revealing he had previous votes against him in an earlier challenge meeting with Ogakor. No doubt the game would have looked mighty different if Skupin had stayed around and its almost a given than both Colby Donaldson and Tina Wesson would not have seen the end of the game like they did.

As serious and scary as Skupin's injury was, the most frightening health scare no doubt in my mind was the one Russell Swan suffered during Survivor Samoa. Just like with what happened in Australia, Swan's Galu tribe had a massive manpower advantage over Russell Hantz' Foa Foa clan. Also like Skupin, Swan was the strongest player on the Galu squad and was the clear leader. So he took the lead during what was a truly gut wrenching challenge where teammates were blindfolded as they maneuvered a huge ball through an obstacle course as another teammate inside the ball yelled instructions on how to go through it. As the challenge proceeded, it became obvious that Russell was having great difficulty as he began to stumble around. While still blindfolded, he hunched over at one point to try and catch his breath. The second part of the challenge was where the blindfolded tribe members would have to steer a ball though a maze, with one person standing at each corner. Russell took his spot and than quickly passed out onto the table. Probst immediately stopped the challenge and rested him down on the ground as medical was brought in. He had been passed out for about five seconds and according to the medical personnel, his blood pressure had dropped very low. As the two tribes were instructed to go back to camp, Swan was sat up in order to see how he would respond. He proceeded to pass out again but this time with his eyes open as it looked like he had stopped breathing and was lifeless. You could see the immense concern on Probst's face as Swan was once again put down on his back. The call was made to officially remove him from the game as the now alert Swan shook his head in disagreement. The move was just as monumental as the Skupin one as Galu had dominated the game to that point and had decimated the Foa Foa tribe. Swan kept the tribe in order as the elder statesman who was also a brutally strong competitor. However his absence caused things to quickly spiral out of control for Galu, who without their leader to keep them in line, began to turn on one another as they foolishly voted out Eric first during the inaugural merged TC, instead of picking off the four remaining Foa Foa members. Russell Hantz of course was one of those four Foa Foa members and combined with his brilliant use of the hidden immunity idol, unbelievably helped bring that foursome all the way to the end of the game, where Natalie White won it all. The Skupin and Swan injuries were the biggest ever in Survivor history and no doubt were clear evidence of just how much they can alter the course of a given season.

One of the more lighthearted and comical injuries well cemented in Survivor lore took place in season 4 Marquesas when John Carroll got stung by a sea urchin and needed someone to pee on his hand to dull the pain and fight off the venom. After Paschal English failed due to performance anxiety, good old Kathy Vavrick-O'Brien came to the rescue and popped a squat successfully. John turned out to be all right but he proved that even the waters of Survivor are treacherous (Richard Hatch getting bitten by the shark anyone?).

As rough as Survivor can be, luckily there have been no deaths associated with it to this point which is a huge relief. The Russell Swan episode was likely as close as a contestant has ever come to the ultimate finish as he said during the reunion show that season that he believes he was on his way to some sort of afterlife as everything was taking place. However his scary episode certainly reinforces the notion that Survivor is as real as it gets and that the harsh elements of the game can take down even the strongest player at a moment's notice.

CHAPTER 9:   SURVIVOR 101-MY FOOLPROOF PLAN TO WIN THE GAME IF YOU ARE LUCKY ENOUGH TO END UP ON SURVIVOR

It has been a goal of mine to be on Survivor all the way through the 20-plus season run of the show but so far to this point I am still waiting for my shot (paging Mr. Prosbt.....I am waiting by the phone for your call). However I haven't given up and hopefully by the time you are reading this, I will be waving to you from some exotic beach location halfway around the world. In the meantime, I figure I have to continue to sharpen my Survivor skills and strategies for when I do hopefully make it out there and if it doesn't wind up being me, than maybe someone else out there can take the information I have gathered over all these years and use the following methods to help them win the million bucks. I will take a 10 percent commission fee on the winnings so be sure to ask for my address where you can mail me the check. In any event, here are some of my foolproof strategies for how to deal with any and all of the classic Survivor situations that might arise, along with my own ideas and manipulations that will help get your name on the winner's check.

1. LAY LOW EARLY ON AND WORK YOUR ASS OFF: This sounds pretty straight-forward which it really is. The most proven method for early success on Survivor is to get up on the beach, keep your mouth shut, and than get your hands dirty as you do whatever you can to help build the shelter. Every season we find at least one castaway pop off about stupid things or complain about the heat, the bugs, everyone else, etc. and invariably they are the first to head for home. In a game where everyone is a complete stranger to one another, first impressions are everything and if you expose yourself right off the bat as a loudmouth who makes people uncomfortable when you speak, than there is an easy excuse put out there to get rid of you. Its as simple as that and its not rocket science. Some people just can't help themselves though and no doubt the harsh climate can bring out the worst in people. However this is where you have to bite your lip and keep your head down. The less attention you draw to yourself the better.

The second part of this is becoming a worker bee. Building the shelter is obviously the first thing that needs to be done when the tribes hit the beach and this is a prime opportunity for your to show how hard of a worker you are. Even if you don't know what a hammer is, do something to make it seem like you are busy at the task at hand. With shelter being of chief importance in the always rainy climates that Survivor brings contestants to each season, the rest of the group will quickly get fed up with those who are not contributing in this regard.

2. DO NOT...AND I REPEAT...DO NOT IMMEDIATELY START LOOKING FOR THE HIDDEN IMMUNITY IDOL

By now we all know that the hidden immunity idol is a staple on Survivor and that there will be one somewhere near the camps for both tribes right from the get go. Although its incredibly tempting to try your best to find it as quickly as possible, you must refrain from doing this as best you can. We have seen now in the last two seasons how those who immediately went looking for the idol (Kristina in Redemption Island and Christine in South Pacific) quickly put big red marks on themselves due to their acts of Survivor aggression and were thus tossed aside right away. Let someone else get themselves in trouble which keeps you out of the limelight. Yes the rewards of finding it are huge but the consequences of simply looking for it are even larger.

3. GET IN TIGHT WITH THE ALPHA MALE/FEMALE IN THE

TRIBE: A Survivor tribe is just like a pack of wild gorillas. There is always an alpha male or female who quickly takes charge of things and proceeds to lead the tribe from that point forward. You don't want to be this person since oftentimes the leader gets cast aside right before or after the merge which has happened too many times to count on Survivor. However you do want to form a positive relationship with this person in an attempt to get yourself some protection. Just look at how Natalie White hooked on with Russell Hantz in Samoa. That made her a million bucks when it was all said and done as Russell took the hits out front and Natalie collected the pieces from behind. It is a tried and true method for success in the game and it works for both males and females. You want to show that you can be a loyal follower and go along with the alpha male or females program. Anyone outside of the loop will be sent home before the merge arrives.

4. FIND THAT ONE PERSON YOU TRUST MORE THAN ANYONE AND MAKE THAT YOUR ONE TRIED AND TRUE ALLIANCE: I am very leery in advocating a player making an alliance on day 1 as its not enough time for you to really get to know someone and whether or not they are suitable to go far in the game with. We saw this mistake made in Australia when Tina Wesson had to turn her back on Marilyn Hershey after making a pact to watch each other's backs early on. Marilyn couldn't keep up in challenges and became a clear liability. We also saw this in Nicaragua when Holly Hoffman made a day 1 pact with Wendy DeSmidt-Kohlhoff who quickly annoyed the rest of the tribe with her incessant talking. Holly had to abandon ship right away was Wendy was sent home on day 3.

So you can see that making a knee-jerk alliance right away is not always the best idea. The first three days should be about discovering who the one person in your tribe is who can be trustworthy and has good values. Usually those who are married with kids make great alliance members as they have a sense of personal responsibility to play somewhat ethically since they have a family watching from home. However you have to make sure this other person doesn't have physical or personal liabilities that could make them an early target for dismissal because than you are going nowhere with it. It is this person you want to go all the way with.

5. HOW TO HANDLE A MERGE: The merge is always a scary time in Survivor because the game is about to get really intense as both tribes will be joining up in one camp for a free-for-all of scheming. This is a very crucial moment as a player and what happens at that first TC will go a long way in determining how your chances will play out. For one, if the tribes are tied going in, don't even think about jumping ship. We all saw how much guff Cochran got for pulling his Benedict Arnold impression and that alone destroyed his chances of winning the game. The reason jumping ship is such a dumb move is because you will instantly lose all of the support from the tribe you are turning your back on who will now be making up the majority of the jury as your new mates pick them off one by one as what happened in South Pacific. These people would rather give the money to anyone else than a turncoat which is seen as the lowest of the low when it comes to unspeakable Survivor strategies. It is a horrible move all the way around and is a sure fire way to eliminate every chance you have of winning the game.

Now if you end up on the tribe that comes up on the short end of the stick in breaking the merge deadlock, than you have carte blanch to do whatever you can from that point on to get yourself back into the game and that includes making a deal with the other side. Once that deadlock has been broken, you and your remaining tribe members have to realize that there is no sense anymore in spouting the loyalty card. The only option you have left is to scramble as best you can and everyone should realize this. Its self-preservation at this point.

On the flip side, if you end up on the advantage side of the numbers, than ride it out with your tribe until the other group is wiped out. Even if you feel like you are the sixth person of the six, turning your back on the group is a poison pill that will do nothing for your chances to win the game. What you want to do is start planting the seeds to the other weaker members of the six that the alpha leaders of the group need to be stopped before they get to the finals or else they will win easily. This has been a big time strategy in the past and it works. Whoever the leader of the alliance is, that person is the one that needs to be attacked when it gets down to the final six since they have the game wrapped up due to their taking the lead in a method that eliminated a whole other tribe. This is your best path to success at this point in the game.

6. WHAT TO DO IF YOU FIND THE HIDDEN IMMUNITY IDOL: If you are lucky enough to find a hidden immunity idol during the course of the game, resist the urge to let anyone else know you have it. The hidden idol is the ultimate weapon of protecting yourself from attacks from other tribe members and it's a safeguard to use in case of an emergency. If you let other people know you have it, it eliminates this sense of security and in the process might force the rest of the group to vote for you in order to flush it out. That's why you alone need to know that you have the idol and nobody else. It is a priceless weapon to own so don't destroy its effectiveness by letting the cat out of the bag.

7. POST-MERGE, START ALIGNING WITH WEAKER PLAYERS OR PLAYERS WHO WONT LOOK SO GOOD IN FRONT OF THE JURY: If you are still in the game after the merge, than it becomes imperative that you start surrounding yourself with two other players who are physically weaker or who have created ill will around camp and thus will have a tough time earning votes in front of a jury. Hopefully that person you formed the original alliance with early in the game is someone who is not a monster physically but make sure they are not disliked. You obviously want to stick with that person to the end of the game like I suggested, but the other person has to absolutely be someone who has no chance of winning a jury vote. In other words, this person has to be Albert Destrade of South Pacific. Thus you have already given yourself a 50/50 chance of winning the million bucks by going up against your fellow alliance members and those odds are what you would take any day of the week and twice on Sunday. If you can do even better and bring another negative or unworthy person to the finale, than you have to gauge whether turning your back against that alliance member is not going to cause an overall negative feeling toward you in front of the jury. Remember that the jury members hang out with one another at Ponderosa so the talk will get out. If its too much a risk, try the flip of the coin scenario and go with it.

7. **HOW YOU WANT TO HANDLE BEING IN FRONT OF THE JURY:** You have made it all the way to the end of the game and you are sitting there in front of the jury ready to state your case as to why you should win the million dollars and the title as Survivor's overall champ. This is a very crucial moment as many players in the past have blown their shot right

than and there (Clay in Thailand anyone????). You have to be prepared going in for taking heat from the jury who will be sore for not being there in your place with a shot to win the dough. The speech you will give to them is incredibly crucial and it should be your way of arguing why in fact you should be rewarded for your effort. Use this time to describe your strategy and how you implemented it into the game. Talk about why you feel you deserve it over the other two and how you stood out over them. Discuss every single thing you did in the game that was positive or that would go with what a Survivor winner should look like. Remind the jury about how much work you did at camp, how good you were at challenges, how you found the hidden immunity idols, etc. This is your chance to convince them you are the right person to give the money to when it comes to them making their pick. Look into all of the jury members eyes as you are saying this. Try and connect with them if you can. This is your moment and you can't let it go by the wayside.

Once the speeches are over, the jury gets their chance of course to ask some tough questions and make you squirm in your seat. Its very important at this point to remain composed and not to get combative. A combative finalist is a sure fire loser as we saw with Clay in Thailand and Russell in Heroes vs. Villains. You might as well just leave the stage and save the jury the effort of ignoring you outright due to your combative nature. Respect each question and give it as thoughtful and truthful an answer as you can get. If you get asked a question where you have to admit you lied, the best course of action is to cop to it and move on. Trying to dodge the question or hem and haw is a sure fire way to lose a vote. Admitting a past sin in front of everyone will score you more points in front of the jury than anything. In the end, its your answers that will likely determine whether you win the money and you don't want to regret it later if you wound up dropping the ball there because its completely in your control to give the jury what they want to hear. As long as you answer their questions as best you can, there is nothing more that can be done. If you still lose the final vote than it just wasn't meant to be.

So there it is. I spelled it all our for your prospective Survivor contestants to win the game and bask in your newfound million dollar riches. It sounds so simple but every season we see players trip up and violate these most simple Survivor rules and they go down in flames as a result. The game is difficult no doubt but being prepared for every situation will have you better prepared to make these correct moves along the way.

CHAPTER 10: SURVIVOR SEASON RANKS AND SOME TOP TEN LISTS UP FOR DEBATE

BEST PLAYERS EVER

1. Rob Mariano
2. Sandra-Diaz Twine
3. Richard Hatch
4. Parvati Shallow
5. Ozzy Lusth
6. Russell Hantz
7. Tom Westman
8. Amanda Kimmel
9. JT Thomas
10. Coach

MOST HATED

1. Russell Hantz
2. Johnny Fairplay
3. Shannon Elkins

4. Parvati Shallow

5. Richard Hatch

6. Rob Cesternino

7. Jerri Manthey

8. Marty Piombo

9. Coach

10. Randy Bailey

MOST LIKED

1. Rupert Boneham

2. Ethan Zohn

3. Ozzy Lusth

4. Colby Donaldson

5. Tom Westman

6. Stephenie LaGrossa

7. Jenna Morasca

8. Cirie Fields

9. Rudy Boesch

10. Roger Bingham

BEST STRATEGIC GAMES

1. Rob Mariano

2. Rob Cesternino

3. Russell Hantz

4. Todd Herzog

5. Parvati Shallow

6. Cirie Fields

7. Todd Herzog

8. Richard Hatch

9. Cochran

10. Jim Rice

BEST CHALLENGE PLAYERS

1. Ozzy Lusth

2. Rob Mariano

3. Tom Westman

4. Terri Deitz

5. Parvati Shallow

6. Colby Donaldson

7. Sophie Clarke

8. Jud "Fabio" Birza

9. JT Thomas

10. Kelly Wigglesworth

BEST SURVIVOR SEASONS IN ORDER

1. Heroes VS. Villains

2. All Stars

3. Borneo

4. Micronesia

5. Amazon

6. Palau

7. Australia

8. Samoa

9. Tocantins

10. Pearl Islands

11. Africa

11. Redemption Island

13. China

14. South Pacific

15. Gabon

16. Guatemala

17. Vanuatu

18. Marquesqas

19. Fiji

20. Panama

21. Cook Islands

22. Thailand

23. Nicaragua

About The Author: Michael Keneski is a freelance writer who lives in Long Island, New York with his wife Allison and son Ryan.

46218674R00087

Made in the USA
Lexington, KY
24 July 2019